# Contents

# Acknowledgment

## Tessie Mae Morrison Calhoun
### June 12, 1919–February 19, 1983

*I write in honor of my mother whose quiet example provides the motivation for my enduring purpose.*

*This tribute to my mother is offered as an inspiration to all my nieces and nephews in her memory.*

Most people don't grow up. Most people age. They find parking spaces, honor their credit cards, get married, have children, and call that maturity. What that is, is aging.

—*Maya Angelou*

# In the Shadow of Sacrifice Thoughts on Life and Success

**HOWARD CALHOUN**

New Hanover County Public Library
201 Chestnut St.
Wilmington, NC 28401

**Librika Publishing LLC**
**Pikeville, NC 27863**

For more information contact:
Librika Publishing
PO Box 1176
Mount Olive NC  28365-1176
librikamedia@gmail.com
www.librikamedia.com

Publisher's Cataloging-in-Publication
(Provided by Quality Books, Inc.)

Calhoun, Howard.
    In the shadow of sacrifice : thoughts on life and success/Howard Calhoun.
        p. cm.
    Essays.
    Includes index.
    LCCN 2013937379
    ISBN 978-1-938348-00-6 (hardcover)
    ISBN 978-1-938348-02-0 (softcover)
    ISBN 978-1-938348-01-3 (ePUB)
    ISBN 978-1-938348-03-7 (ePDF)

    1. Calhoun, Howard.   2. Counselors—United States—Biography   3. Success.   I Title.

BF636.6.C35 2013                361'.06'092
                                QBI13-600062

Dust Jacket/Cover Design: David Cain, Cain Galleries, Goldsboro NC

# Preface

I just didn't want to think about it but it kept coming back into my mind. My reasons to continue resisting got weaker and weaker. Finally, I was cornered and out of alibis.

I had to tell my story. To relive the journey. To write it down. To share it with those on journeys of their own.

This book is the culmination of experiences carved out of the benefit of my mother's marathon sacrifice. My disposition and how I process life are straight from my mother's textbook on living. Although I vacillated and fought hard against writing it, it was my mother's sacrifice—and the sacrifice of many generations before her—that won out in the end. It is from her that I derived the courage and resilience to step forward. It is because of her I am afforded the opportunity to share my stories and thoughts as healthy anecdotes, despite the harmful constants of poverty, abuse, and insecurity that underscore my memories.

I am convinced that—while paying tribute to my mother's life— this book will enrich the lives of many and take them on a ride through the innermost hopes and fantasies of a young, challenged child surrounded by a large, tight-knit family, and an even tighter community of freewheeling disciplinarians. Amidst backwardness, illiteracy, and underemployment, it will plow through the anxieties and fears of the teen years and capture the hopes, aspirations, disappointments, and successes of adulthood. Readers will get a picture of naiveté, straightforwardness, and complexities—all sorted and distilled in an orderly maze called life and traversing a broad range of topics and ideas.

At its core, it is a loving homage to my mother's epic sacrifice. She knew and accepted that her situation didn't have a silver lining and yet, in the shadow of her unearned suffering, nestled a cocoon worthy of her laying it all on the line. Without her sacrifice, I most likely would be too disturbed to assemble any stories, especially those without anger, bitterness, and hatred. Her sacrifice and the manner in which she sacrificed spawned these wholesome stories. From my father's moods and actions, I was hit with endless challenges. It is my mother, however, who taught me not only how to handle his moods but the moods and challenges of the world as well. She provided the inspiration and the remedy.

# Introduction

A lifetime is but a series of moments woven into slices of human-interest stories known only to the person who is doing the telling. The storyteller flashes in and out of scenarios, adding and deleting characters and venues without a clear understanding of time's allowances or purposes for a wider audience. Owing irredeemable sacrifice, I am compelled to entrust a bit of me in a lot of you. My thoughts and views are offered as an integral part of my narration; however, they are not presented as authority. They are accessible to promote and encourage contrast, thoughtfulness, and an assessment of your own life.

I believe our thoughts are as much a part of our story as any physical aspect. In fact, I consider our thoughts to represent the truest essence of who we are and—once buried in the hearts and minds of those left behind—they become the only burials worth mentioning. My stories will encourage you to think critically about the significance, purpose, and nature of your own experiences and why I consider stories to be a central part of life.

"We are our stories" is a statement attributed to the ancient Greeks. We all have stories. Although the venues may be unrelated, our similarities emerge and differences trivialize as we start to sort and extrapolate what really matters. By presenting my stories from an environment of sacrifice, I am able to remove myself just enough to assemble a clearer and more meaningful picture of how it all fits. I believe that the more we understand about the developmental aspects of our stories, the better we are able to discern our purpose and contribution to the ongoing story of life.

My father was an aggressive and towering figure who shared many of his thoughts with the rest of the family and me, albeit sometimes in a coercive manner. His thoughts were more of the surface type, and they come through in a lot of my stories. My mother's thoughts and behavior provided the deep, introspective understanding that has guided and shaped me and my interpretations throughout the years. Her love for all was deep and sacred. Her constant meditation often confounded and transfixed me. When I would question her, she would often reply, "I was just thinking." Her deafness sought to make her a casualty in a world defined by sound. Although her level of deafness was severe and noticeable when others attempted to communicate with her, all her children were perfect translators in an unexplainable phenomenon that went well beyond lip reading. In her presence, I always sensed enormous wealth and depth in her perception of the world around her.

I often found myself trying to go there with her. She showed immense courage and faith in how she handled the many adversities that confronted her. In her long bout with cancer, she explained in her usual soft voice that she knew she was not going to beat it, and it was okay. She was basically alerting the family and me that we did not have to keep up the charade of trying to protect her from what she knew.

Her unusual calmness and ease in times of difficulties amazed and comforted me. I never heard her complain, feel sorry for herself, or refer to herself as a victim. No matter what was going on with her, she always greeted others with a warm gesture, pleasant smile, and sincere thankfulness. My mother was the silent mover and shaker in our household, and even Pop stood down on the rare occasions she stood up.

When my father would lose sight of the degree of pain he was inflicting on us, she would say, "That's enough, Gary." And although he would say something like "Stay out of this, woman"—because it was the man thing to say—he would bring the beatings to an immediate halt. She seemed comfortable in the background and cared little about getting her dues when it came to credit for her contribution to the family's welfare. If her love and quietness lured you into misdeeds or you got it twisted, you would abruptly feel her presence. I know this because she had to "get hold of" me a couple of times. She always did it with no additional amps.

As a final thought, I am a little concerned about being in the limelight and out from under the radar. I guess I just can't calm the mother in me. This book is also a commentary and mouthpiece for all the mothers and other caregivers who have made, and are continuing to make, tremendous sacrifices for others. Because of my challenges, I may have needed the shadow to hide just as much as I needed the sacrifice to sprout. You are me, and I am you. You are a product of sacrifice. I invite you out of your shadow. "Thanks, Mom, for the sacrifice and the shadow."

# Soft Negatives®

Life is blistered with many common toxic occurrences, events, and ideas over continuums and across countless venues. Yet they are treated by many in a nonchalant manner, viewed as routine and accepted as the way it is. Consequences are received as necessary tolerances or the price of living. These occurrences, events, and ideas are what I call soft negatives, and they are scattered throughout the stories in this book.

Soft negatives are everyday happenings in life and may be perceived as harmless. Oftentimes they may not be appraised as negatives at all even though they produce negative outcomes. It's that little lie that becomes common, whether told by an individual, the family, the government, or an institution. The cumulative effect over time can be devastating, yet it is never fully accounted for by the many sprinkles that make up its toll. Soft negatives are imbedded in almost every facet of life in such a subtle, nonthreatening, and insignificant manner that in their single form they are almost undetectable. Killing someone using a drop of poison so small that it would require fifty years as opposed to an amount taking only fifty seconds is an example of how soft negatives work. It could be something as simple as that "must-have" barbecue promoted as the best in twelve southern states, or the award-winning education program that only delivers half of a rainbow, yet is endorsed by the federal government and subsidized by the taxpayers. On February 27, 2013, author Michael Moss, appeared on MSNBC and introduced his book Salt Sugar Fat. He explained a neurological connection on how the food giants hook us on junk food. It is another classic example of a soft negative.

So many soft negatives envelop you and me that soft negatives and life appear to be one. I have examined many of them in my stories. As a former schoolteacher and a former school counselor, I was—and I am still—opposed to handouts (i.e., worksheets and answer sheets) because

I believe they hamper initiative, resourcefulness, and innovation. My stories are told in the same manner as I taught and counseled. There is meaning in every story. There are no handouts; you must ponder and probe for that deep, introspective understanding often exhibited by my mother. If the many surface stories of my father, siblings, and friends cause you to lose perspective of whose sacrifice I honor the most, then this story is presented to bring you back to the meditative mission of this book. Also, let us not forget the value of meditation, because all the great prophets, including Buddha, Jesus, and Muhammad spent days and even months in meditation.

Our mindless indulgence and our unfamiliarity with the nature and complexity of soft negatives have needled away from the pursuit of success and happiness in life for many. For others, it has sent and kept them on the wrong ladder in search of success. Included in my stories are many of your stories and, of course, your soft negatives. If you are angered by life's soft negatives, or see soft negatives as impediments that won't show their faces, or as obstacles with two or more faces, you are encouraged to embrace the energy produced by anger and use it as motivation to pursue success as the best revenge. It is as the crow flies, out of my mother's textbook on life.

# Lessons to Learn

Measuring the value of what my siblings and I inherited from our parents according to the size of their wallet, it would lead me to conclude that my parents left us absolutely nothing. My father often used to speak about me "not having two nickels to rub together," and I often wondered if he was referring to himself while trying to take a jab at me. My cousin, Bobby Morrison, wrote a book titled *Bama Boy*, where he depicted almost shameful poverty in reverent terms as he paired it with a genuine, caring, and loving family.

I know you may be saying, "Oh no, not another poor-me story." To the contrary, we were poor, but I am not complaining. It's just a fact, or at least a fact relative to all the other factual markers I learned were indicators of poverty . . . in America. We must have been overqualified for welfare or my father refused to take it, opting instead to allow us to feel the full brunt of what it was to be poor. I often said to myself, he must have been so proud of being poor that he saw himself and poverty as one and didn't want us to ever disown him.

As I got older, I learned he was doing the very best he knew and joked for years to cover the choke of tears. My father would often say he had these kids, and he was going to take care of them. He would say his father walked out on his mother with eight kids; his promise to us was we were going to make it or starve together. I don't know about the rest of my siblings, but there were times I thought he was going to pull off the starving part.

I am the ninth child of a mother who birthed eleven and the tenth child of a father of twelve. I was born in a household that had its origin about four scores beyond the end of slavery in the United States. Growing up, I remember the house as crowded, noisy, sometimes funny, and, oh yeah, smoky. I got a full helping of secondhand smoke a long time before the research trickled down to reveal the ills of smoking. My daddy, being the man of the house, well, he just didn't put his smoking up for a vote.

When I was a child I really didn't have an understanding of the concept of poverty, but not having electricity, food, running water, a refrigerator, a television, a telephone, an automobile, a bicycle, or medical care pretty much summed up our level of wealth. Yet, my oldest brother, Gary Jr., found it necessary to confuse me even more by suggesting we had risen out of poverty by the time I came along, and that we were doing quite well. He went on to explain that when our brother Albert died, all those living almost perished trying to pay for his death. He said Albert's death confirmed to him that we couldn't even afford to die.

Furthermore, since Albert died in his sleep, every time someone fell asleep and it wasn't bedtime, the whole family got nervous. Being nine years his junior, I couldn't argue too much with my brother about our family economic condition during his childhood. But given the descent we were in when I learned about it, I hate to think how we could have gotten any poorer. If we had moved to prison, we would have all sung The Jeffersons' theme song. As a matter of fact, on one occasion, my father came to me in the kitchen while I was making a peanut butter and jelly sandwich and began to scold me about putting two products on one sandwich. He said, "Now, boy, you know we don't have food to waste. You either use peanut butter or jelly, not both of them, and the bread just needs to be glazed over, not stuffed. I done told you about trying to go to that schoolhouse acting like a big shot. Now you take one of them off your sandwich, put it back in the jar, and get out of this kitchen before I skin you alive."

I was torn between looking at my father like he was crazy (of course, I had to use the undercover version of that one) and looking at him like he was Aristotle or Plato. I was waiting for him to blow the covers off history by explaining how society got it all wrong by mixing peanut butter and jelly. I pretended to be in awe and suspected he was on the verge of issuing some ultra-intelligent statement overlooked by researchers for centuries. I never got that. However, I also never questioned his wisdom—I love to smile.

What I did was to use my wisdom. The next day I approached Frankie, a classmate of mine, to embark on an experiment with me where he would bring a peanut butter sandwich and I would bring a jelly sandwich, or vice versa, and we would switch a side of the sandwich so I could have my peanut butter and jelly sandwich without throwing our household into bankruptcy.

So, Gary Jr., if we were doing better, somehow the memo never got to my father; or, during your childhood, the family either hadn't risen to such prominence to afford peanut butter and jelly; or, you were much cleverer than me and never got caught commingling peanut butter and jelly.

# To Be or Not to Be . . . What Is the Position?

How we come into this world is how we go out . . . or is it, who we come into this world *through* and spend time *around* that determines how we go out?

Discussing this has spawned some interesting conversations over the years about the developmental aspects of identities and lots in life. Are identities determined mostly by birth, family, tradition, generationally acquired beliefs, or individually selected beliefs? I will present a few of these beliefs and positions I have encountered, and I will offer my views in support or as a counter. In fact, throughout this book, I will present various topics and positions in a thought-provoking manner. You are encouraged to chime in with your two or three cents' worth to expand the conversations with contributions from your stories.

This first section is an examination in general of what I have observed about the formation of some core beliefs. Now, of course, this does not include all beliefs or all the beliefs I have encountered. Regardless of how these beliefs or positions have been formed, many undoubtedly have assumed ownership without much forethought and evaluation. They tend to defend them often at enormous risk, harm, and grief to themselves. Some vehemently claim they arrived at their beliefs through their own volition, although the evidence supports a different conclusion.

These beliefs and positions often become a part of who they think and believe they are. Just questioning a position can be perceived as an affront to the individual. Exhorting too closely for thoughtfulness about their position usually creates an arsenal of rebuffs, followed by scant explanations. For example, "I am a Democrat because my father and family are Democrats" or "I was born a Baptist and I am going to die a Baptist." If one elects to push further, it may prompt a complete shutdown or a loss of a friendship. Now there are many good reasons to take a stand or hold firm to a particular position, but none avail themselves through laziness and being spoon-fed.

There are those who hold the position of believing in the negative. The position they defend is that something bad is going to happen or it never comes out good or right no matter what they do, say, or try. Yet, these are generally the same people who are perplexed when more positive things do not come their way. On more than a few occasions I have tried to highlight the positive, expecting an affirmation of some type, only to be met with more negativity. My finding has been that they are bigger believers and advocates of their skill deficits rather than their skill assets or potential. Time after time, I have been scolded about my ignorance of their ability, luck, or calling. This appears to be true even if they have had more than their share of subpar experiences.

I don't know how many times I have been enlightened and put in my place to the facts of their life as they stick to their position. My lack of shared understanding of this has kept me at odds with this particular position. This propensity to defend the negative so aggressively has led me to conclude there must be some greater benefit in it for the defender since no "slightly" reasonable person would choose self-destruction over self-construction. It appears this group has lost sight of the value of their abilities, and they are more apt to rely on the position and belief that there are more dividends in their disability than their ability. Could this be the aim of this particular belief and the greater benefit they desire?

There is another category of people who hold beliefs or positions that force me to refer to them as "fly-by-nighters," subject to whatever social or political whim is deemed "in" by whatever source that is "in." They don't have a fixed position on anything and are waiting for someone or something more popular, stronger, or meaningful than they to give them a position. Hence, they will become defenders of whatever the popular fad is until the next political or social wave blows through. Commercial marketers are great at targeting this population. Politicians are masters at capitalizing on this human frailty as well. Year after year, many in this group are taken in by whoever can best package their message and corral the most effective delivery system.

I was reminded of this truism when I was working as a program assistant in the prison system and an inmate attempted to explain that the world was full of followers waiting for somebody to give them their opinions and positions. He asked me to observe him while he ascertained two polar positions from a peer in less than five minutes. After getting the inmate to commit to one position, he went back to the same inmate and asked him how he felt about the opposite position. After only a couple of prompts, the inmate changed his position. When I felt I had been conned, I told the inmate I would choose the person for him to demonstrate his experiment on. I chose an inmate who was sharp on many subjects and someone who did not care much about him. I also chose the subject. It took him more time, but the results were the same.

Finally, there are those who feel cheated in life because they were not born of rich, famous, or well-connected parents. At birth, they were victimized or slighted, and, therefore, society owes them. They believe they are entitled to compensation for that birth neglect. This becomes the cornerstone of their argument and defense of their belief and lot in life. Now, of course, there is some level of validity in the advantages of having powerful family ties and such, but to think of the absence of these alleged advantages as an eternal and insurmountable blight only usurps one's lifetime responsibility at birth. It presupposes that whatever a person is to have is the absolute result of the doings or circumstances of someone or something which came before them. Therefore, all the actions and behaviors of the person from birth and beyond are pointless.

I have concluded these people believe anything or anybody other than themselves are responsible for all of their outcomes in life. They were born pawns and puppets. They are helpless and are being jerked around by forces superior to them as a result of their birth curse. This makes all barriers and challenges legitimate scapegoats and fosters effortless choices and faulty expectations. It makes seeing the light almost impossible. A person holding this belief can forever curse his condition and justify that condition to himself and his family, and go through life never seeing or knowing the wealth within.

The worst of this tyrant is that this belief becomes a pseudo truth that is passed through generations as fact. There is certainly enough evidence to disprove the fallacy of the silver spoon theory, especially if it is being touted as a prerequisite for success. There is also equally enough evidence to prove that complete and abject illiteracy and poverty at birth are no sure determinant for failure in life. My further study of this belief reveals there are more acquired limitations than innate limitations. Self-imposed personal and generational-induced limitations account for limited thinking which, in turn, amounts to limited achievements and, thus, the established reality that is defended so fervently becomes a self-fulfilling prophecy. On the flipside, those who are born of rich, famous, or well-connected parents may flaunt a position of entitlement and superiority just as errant and destructive as those born without those alleged advantages.

# Principal Lesson

I was very glad to get out of R. B. Dean Elementary School and away from the principal, Mr. McBee. I heard my classmates say a lot about him, so as a kid, I guess I learned some things that were not very good and may not have been true. He had a reputation throughout the school as a hard-nosed taskmaster, and everyone knew if you were called to his office it almost certainly meant some type of physical intervention at the end of his paddle or belt.

Although I do not remember him ever getting a'hold of me, I developed a dislike for him based on my peers' remarks. Accordingly, I could not wait to leave his school because I had a few things I wanted to get off my chest (my classmates put them there). I got my chance in the seventh grade about a month after I arrived at Townsend Middle School. Since I was no longer his pupil or under his custody, I thought it was a perfect time to give him a piece of my mind.

On this particular day, I happened to pass him in the hallway, so I turned and yelled back to him, "Hey, McBee!" He turned to inquire as to who was addressing him without a handle on his name. I said, "Yeah, you, McBee." I was confident I was out of his jurisdiction and beyond his reach. I said to myself, "He can't do anything to me because I am no longer his student." Mr. McBee calmly walked up to me, grabbed me by my arm, and said, "Come with me, boy."

I immediately thought he was going to take me to the principal's office where I was going to get a chance to plead my case (lie) about what happened. Instead, he ushered me into the nearest open vacant room, took off his belt, and commenced to whip me as if I had stolen something. The entire time he was asking me, "What's my name? What's my name?" I felt like I was Floyd Patterson or Ernie Terrell, and he was Muhammad Ali trying to beat Cassius Clay out of me. It happened so fast I could not get my wits about myself, so I just started stammering and telling him he did not have the right to do what he was doing. Not until I called him Mr. McBee did he let up on the beating. He sent me out like I was a missionary and told me to go back and tell all my classmates what he did to me. Furthermore, I was to tell them that we were always to address him as Mr. McBee, even if we were in college.

Mr. McBee walked out of the school without telling the principal or anyone what he did to me. Of course, I was so outdone and embarrassed that if my classmates did not know, this was one lesson I decided they would learn as I did. How ironic that I could complete six years at his school without ever feeling his belt, only to feel its sting for the first time a little over four months after I graduated elementary school. I guess I couldn't leave well enough alone. He has been deceased for many years, but for all my classmates and others who don't know, he is still Mr. McBee.

# Are You Smarter Than a Sixth Grader?

There seems to be a lot of researched-based parenting programs purporting a high degree of success, although I have yet to find one offering a guarantee. Many explain that the success rates are connected to the most appropriate model selected for the individual client or family, and it must be implemented with fidelity. Some claim better maintenance of behavior and sustained gains after the six-month follow-up. Doctorate or master-level clinicians develop many of these models.

I have one question and hope it is proper and fitting. If parents with a sixth-grade education or less reared you and the results indicated you and your siblings turned out okay, why would you not use your parents' model with your children? Harvard graduate Judge Lynn Toler of Divorce Court wrote a book titled "My Mother's Rules" where she cites and credits her mother's rules of emotional management as a guide in handling many erratic challenges. According to the research, I must find the most appropriate program, so while I am going through the gamut of models trying to find the right one, my child is forced to wait or go with a model that may not be the most appropriate.

I know one size does not fit all, but from my oldest sister (who was born in the '40s) to my youngest sister (who was born in the '60s), there is a generational difference, so I suspect you could say they were born in different eras or different days. Nevertheless, my parents stayed fast to their way with both of them, and the results are similar. If the model works, why look away from that model for another entirely different program?

My elementary school principal made a comment once that I never forgot, even though I was nothing more than a child myself. He said there was something about those country boys that made them easier to manage than those city boys. It was years later in life when I understood what he meant. He was referring to a parenting model of rearing that had sustained gains well beyond any six-month follow-up program, and it was measurable and more prevalent in the rural community. However, there were no credentials behind the developers of these models and no money to be made from the duping of the research.

Our structured rearing has made us more amenable to the structured environment of the classroom. The new day's technical and legal scare has forced many parents to back away from tried-and-true methods of parenting in favor of laboratory and controlled studies. Presence, love, structure, consistency, and congruence pretty much summed up the model of rearing for my siblings and me. If, as a child, I pushed and tried to insert my "new day" approach or affront to my parents' sixth-grade education level techniques, I was always reminded, consistently, that if my place of stay was the same today as it was yesterday, and I was not the one responsible for the pay, then there was no way my say was going to get any play.

Yes, things do change and sometimes things that were effective many years ago may not be as effective or even practical today. So updates can be useful, but not just for the sake of change. It must be necessary and only in the amount necessary. It should complement or enhance your parents' model if that model has a good track record. If it changes the basic structure of your parents' model, it is probably another model and should be viewed with some trepidation. Keep it simple. Those parents who decided, even before having children, they would never be like their parents even if they had turned out all right, left the track and the entire station years before it became necessary. They are the victims of offspring bias. By committing to "anything but my parents' model," they forced themselves and their families to start from scratch.

By the time they learned or recognized that their parents may have had more sense than their former education attested to, irreparable damage to their children may have already been done. In an attempt to stay current with the times and not be labeled "old-school" parents, these parents, more committed to disproving their parents' models than rearing their children, work harder searching the Internet and global market for answers that may have eluded them in their homes. Professionals and the media constantly remind parents of their poor parenting skills, and, in turn, their parenting confidence has plummeted.

Looking for a manual has replaced the standard of enduring necessary mistakes in the effort and growth of becoming a good parent. Some have succumbed to the suggestions and advice of their children for the most viable option and model for the rearing of their children. Good luck with that one. Some parenting models may only be capable of mimicking structure and congruence; therefore, they may produce products, unmindful and unfamiliar with real-life structure. Some children from these programs have found the schools, workplaces, and social arena problematic to the point that possibilities and productivity are unobtainable, or at the least severely hampered. Those who are inexperienced or have no experience in playing by the rules are forced out and resort to taking on society using their own rules obtained from absent parenting or by-standing parenting. The challenges and barriers for them will be greater and to be fair, if they somehow find a way to overcome them, their rewards will probably be greater also. However, the odds of success are against them and the level, magnitude, and number of failures are potentially greater.

Parents who left the parenting station (lack of presence), left their children unattended (lack of love), without any guidance (lack of structure), and in a haphazard manner (lack of consistency) have provided an example unworthy of comparison to a good sixth-grade model regardless of their education level. Many parenting models target the wayward behaviors of children and young adults. Because models may align themselves with what most insurance and third-party payers will reimburse for their services, these models, as great as they may be, become systemic victims, and must overcome the negative effect of a more ingrained bad model from birth. I have seen too many capable parents so concerned with the way their children might view or measure them and their actions relative to parenting that they become hesitant, unsure, immobile, and inconsistent. How did their children become the most qualified agents to evaluate their parenting skills? So, the parents placate and acquiesce, hoping somehow this demonstrates love and their children will love them more for it and work harder to please them.

This somewhat innocent-appearing parenting style or strategy permits it to linger "as not so bad" for years; hence, there is no need to examine it for ill effects. The observation of a child in wrongdoing is by-standing parenting. The failure to qualify the contextual inappropriateness of behavior (e.g., fast running on the track may be encouraged and praised but fast running in the hallway or in someone's establishment is discouraged), well, you get the picture. There may be nothing wrong with an action when paired in the proper venue. Not seizing these teachable moments are examples of consent and upholding a child in inappropriateness. Abstaining or defending inappropriate behavior and renaming it "standing up for my child" nullify the importance of positions and teach a brand of loyalty that threatens to put the whole family in jail. Not only does a child deserve to be cautioned on what not to do, a child also must be taught by example what to do and encouraged to engage in age-appropriate behavior. The child must be exposed to an environment that challenges his or her interests, aptitude, and development. Boundaries must be pushed in a healthy manner. The guidance of appropriate parenting is important to healthy growth and development.

I have learned all of this from my sixth-grade educated parents. Is great parenting synonymous with complex models? Not necessarily. Can a sixth-grader's model be bad? Yes. It is the content of the character of the modeler that matters the most. Could it be we have been intentionally and strategically moved away from the simple sixth-grader's model in order to make room for capital investments in a new area called "Parent Management"? Standards are being developed by advanced degree professionals to promote these paid clinicians (incongruence) as the new experts to replace even grandma's parenting. Based solely on the results and outcomes of today's parents with the support and services of the paid expert versus the era of the sixth-grade educated parent without the expert, are we really smarter than a sixth grader?

# Principles

We hear a lot about people having strong principles and taking tough positions in life like those of the framers of this country. "Give me liberty or give me death." Where are these men today? I say they are still here. I call them principle pretenders. These framers were men of courage, skills, and cleverness, but maybe not as principled as one might think.

Now what I am going to say is not inclusive of every framer of this country and does not negate the fact that they were men of tremendous courage and vision. Some may argue they were men of their times and the economics and pressures of that era robbed these men of some of their character. There were some settlers of that time who maintained the highest character and were true to their principles; however, for expediency, some modified or abandoned their positions to advance their cause. At the end of the day, these were the ones who carried the day.

Their greatness now has to be forever confined to the fact they chose exile to persecution. What greater sacrifice and more principled position can men take and believe so strongly in than the willingness to leave the land of their birth and renounce their citizenship rather than to keep living under persecution and tyranny? Taking such a position makes one want to stand and applaud. That same group of people who were willing to risk treason and certain death by the mother country, who shed their blood and the blood of others to throw off the shackles of oppression, also authored an attempted genocide of one race, the persecution and enslavement of another, and the ostracism of a gender. These were learned men so I don't think we can chalk this one up to a bunch of illiterates. What it does say is that maybe they were not as for or as against a position as we might have thought. Maybe they had only one position with two parts? They were against being persecuted, but the position to oppress and persecute others—well, that was up for consideration. The reason I concluded they weren't as principled as history professes is because of their willingness to establish and support a system of persecution with the understanding and knowledge of an inherent wrongness imbued with atrocities reminiscent of their recent history. These principled men, at least in this calling, shrank from their responsibility.

Men are not strange; they just attempt to placate their ignorance on the ignorance of others. That action or inaction by our Founding Framers ushered in one of the greatest periods of hypocrisy known to man. Yet history, careful not to cast shadows on their greatness, glosses over it and treats it as blameless and victimless. I have heard it passed off that both groups were victims of a horrible and terrible system. Even if it were true, they knew enough about the wrongness of persecution, being fresh from the persecution of Europe, to say, "no mas, no mas" for themselves and their families. It was either too bad for them, or they believed they were too good for it. They passed it on with little or no remorse, citing their light and plight as part of their inalienable right. We must assign that blight to their greatness.

Is it plausible for this country to have risen to such greatness so rapidly without the exact action of its founders given the era and the precarious nature and conditions inherent by any new nation? I guess the answer to that question may never be known. What does seem apparent is this great nation appears to continue to reel to some degree from that defect in vision as evident by the current division in Washington, and it may still yet serve as a catalyst to our demise. Some early sanctioned alignments have contributed to unity along various other "isms," i.e., sex, religion, race, and nationality—while concurrently ensuring separatism where it concerned Americanism. I will not keep beating this horse, but I think all of us share and understand the ramifications in the principle of a house divided against itself that was issued by a great American who keeps a symbolic shadowy watch in Washington.

# Don't You Dare . . . Call It Puppy Love

The year was 1965. The month was December. The Beatles released Rubber Soul. Charles de Gaulle was re-elected as France's president. "A Charlie Brown Christmas" debuted on CBS. And another Brown named James was belting out the R&B chart toppers "Papa's Got a Brand New Bag" and "I Feel Good," which was pretty much where I was at the time. However, as Fantasia would say, it was a little bittersweet because the joy of the Christmas break was spoiled by its length; therefore, it needed to hurry up and end so I could be whole again.

Ms. Bullard, my third-grade teacher, had taken a liking to me, and I was in love with her, too. It always bothered me when a student was mean to her or gave her a hard time. My job was to love and protect her, and I always worked hard to do everything I could to please her. She and I were to get married and live happily ever after. All she had to do was to wait, let's see, ten years until I turned 18, and it would all be legal. I did as much as I could for her. I volunteered to pick up the trash, passed out papers, etc. I would take on the biggest guy in the class for her.

As I said earlier, I was sort of happy about the holiday break, but I was also sad because I knew it would be about two weeks before I could really smile again. Sure, I ran, jumped, and played like all the other kids, but I was a little different from them because I was in love. Besides, if I was lucky, the only thing my brother and I would get for Christmas would be a cap pistol with one roll of caps; once that roll was gone, we would have to pistol-whip each other to win a gunfight. At least I didn't have to worry about a tragedy at the hands of that gun if I felt I couldn't take it any longer from being away from the love of my life.

New Year's came and went, and I was beginning to feel a little better about 1966. The Beatles album went on to top the chart for six weeks, and James Brown collected a Grammy for his brand-new bag. All U.S. cigarette packs had to carry the warning, "Caution: Cigarette smoking may be hazardous to your health." Transit workers were striking in New York City, and there were protests throughout the United States and around the world against the Vietnam War, but all I wanted or cared about was getting back to school to see my future wife.

I believe I returned to school on Monday, January 3, 1966, and it was one of the happiest days of my life until Ms. Bullard's announcement: "Class, I have something wonderful to tell you. My name is now Mrs. Thomas."

I thought to myself, "Who is Mrs. Thomas and what does that mean for us?" Then she told us she got married over the Christmas holiday. I did not know what to do. I wanted to cry, but I was too angry to make any noise. I was stunned. I had thought about her all during the Christmas holiday and could not wait until it was over so I could see her again, and she spent her holiday getting married! How could she have done that to me? I refused to call her Mrs. Thomas, and I would not answer when she called on me.

It was my first exercise in participating in a strike. I was finished volunteering to help her pick up trash or hand out papers. I said to myself, "After what she did to me, she does not have to speak to me again." I could not believe she wanted me to call her somebody else's name. I decided I was not going to do it, and she could not make me. I was also not going to work hard in her class any more to make good grades for her because she did not care about me. The last half of my year was filled with less happiness than the first, because I believed Ms. Bullard had told me she was going to wait for me and she did not keep her word. I did not know a lot in the third grade, but I knew enough to know that Mrs. Thomas did not sound like Mrs. Calhoun. As for that puppy or mushy love, that wasn't me, because my love for Ms. Bullard was solid . . . as a rock.

# Hog Wild

Too often when it was my time to feed the hogs, I would forget. I guess their eating was not important to me. When my father learned of this, he came up with a rule: "Whenever you feel a need to eat, go feed the hogs. Now, if you don't ever eat, you don't ever have to feed the hogs." I believed this caused me to have some bias and partiality toward the hogs, because it appeared my father was putting the hogs and their needs on an even footing with me and my needs. Of course, the hogs did not have anything to do with that. On more than a few occasions, however, I thought I should have gotten more out of them than pork, and I was completely unaware of what it required of them to *become* pork.

So, consistent with how this child thought, I concluded a free ride every now and then was more important than pork and the least the hogs owed me for me having to visit them early in the morning and sometimes late at night. Occasionally, my brother Lenwood a.k.a. Head, Cousin John, and I would try to saddle up (I mean go bareback) for a little ride. I must say we had some of the most uncooperative hogs I had ever seen. ("Green Acres" could have never gotten an Arnold from our bunch.) I used to think that they were so ill-willed, after I had given them a good meal (slop) from some of the worst leftover garbage I could find in our house, that they would not stand still so I could get a ride.

This forced me to do it their way. We would lure them (trick them as if we cared about them being hungry) with a bucket of feed to an area favorable for a ride, and while they had their heads down, one of us would sneak up behind and mount the back or come off a banister and flop on the hog's back. Now that last feat was a little tricky, especially if the hog noticed you trying to jump on his back. All I can say is that missing the hog's back could mean a painful contact with where the hog was or an embarrassing introduction to the hog's lifestyle of slop, mud, and manure.

At times, I would find a hog that would allow me to walk up and pet him. The ride was separate, however, so I would still have to mount quickly and find myself off just as quick, which was not much different from a ride after a chase. I never found a hog that really wanted me to ride him, and sometimes, depending on how I was thrown, he did not have to worry about me trying to ride him again. I was not in the business of trying to tame or break a hog. I was mostly concerned about not allowing the hog to break me. I guess I should have been satisfied with the pork chop sandwich.

There were also those occasions when I had to take part in catching a hog, or at least steer a hog or pig into another section of the pen. I remember asking my father once why we had to move the hogs from a sloppy area of the pen to a dryer area. Didn't they like slop? And besides, all they are going to do was mess it up again. He asked why I eat, since all I was going to do was get hungry again. If I wasn't sharp enough to read between the lines and get his point, he would follow it up with something else I needed to decipher, such as, "Son, you shouldn't have to eat a whole hog before you know you are eating pork." Any time I tried to slip, my father would remind me that he had the book in his pocket. Well, my father is shooting off one-liners he thinks I should understand while I was stuck in a hog pen with uncooperative hogs I didn't understand. I just wondered if he had anything in that book in his pocket that would help me get stubborn hogs into a chute so we could take them to the market. Maybe the hogs had some inside information from Milken or Boesky because even the friendly hogs seemed to fight going to the market.

One time my cousin John got his hands on one and was determined he was going to hold on no matter what. He did very well until the hog dragged him into a tree. The next thing I knew, he was a little groggy and had to be led out of the pen. On another occasion, I was involved in moving pigs from their mother for their initiation surgery (neutering). To do this, I had to tag-team and be quick. While a partner distracted the sow, I swooped in and picked up two pigs and was moving very swiftly. As I was exiting the fence, however, their snouts hit the electric fence. All of a sudden, I had electricity running through my body and I had to let those hot pigs go.

The adults thought my behavior was hilarious and wondered why I didn't hold onto them until I got beyond the fence. I did not know how long the electricity was going to continue vibrating through my body, and I was not about to hold on to find out. Besides, the sow was in hot pursuit and closing fast. She was also acting like she cared more about her little ones than she did about the electric fence. I felt it best to give the pigs back to her, clear the fence, and put as much room between the sow and me as possible. Well, given my shocking and electrifying experience, I probably should not have dropped those piglets on the fence. On second thought, these were probably some of the same hogs I had to get up early in the morning to feed, so you would think after all the things we'd been through together, they should have been glad to give me a little ride. Maybe that little jolt of electricity was in order. Perhaps I still have unresolved issues about the hog ride.

# Respect

What is respect? It may be a feeling or attitude of admiration and deference toward somebody or something. It could be consideration toward somebody or something. Now, of course, there are many other things that may be included in the definition of respect, but mostly it involves an intangible quality connected to feelings and attitudes that garnish a sense of a person recognizing and acknowledging another person or thing with honor or regard. The definition appears simple enough to understand regardless of which one a person ascribes to. Yet, from day care to senior care, there seem to be more violators than compliers. The misunderstanding or reckless disregard for this one word has been the impetus for dissolutions of valued long-term relationships, gang afflictions, civil unrest, and national and world wars.

When I was a school counselor, the first phrase that came out of the mouths of the students was, "That student (or teacher or administrator) disrespected me." When I talked with parents, it would be, "They disrespected my son (or daughter)" or "They were disrespectful to me." Teachers would say that a student was disrespectful. It seems everyone knew disrespect when they saw it or felt it, but very few knew much about respect. As a prison and probation official, I heard, "That inmate/guard/probation officer disrespected me." All would say, "Mr. Calhoun, no one is going to disrespect me and get away with it." The student would say, "I would rather take a week or year at home than to have a student or teacher disrespect me." The inmate would say, "I will do ten, twenty years, or even life before I have someone disrespect me."

From the poorhouse to the White House and whether they are in the outhouse or the penthouse, there seems to be nothing more important than respect. Everyone seems to be trying to get that elusive respect. The student chooses to be sent home over staying in school due to disrespect, and gets home and is disrespected at home and chooses to be put out of the house rather than be disrespected. When he is disrespected in the community, he chooses juvenile detention instead of being disrespected, and finally, he chooses solitary lockup rather than stay in the regular prison population and be disrespected.

I have had long conversations with this same student-type in an old grey-headed inmate still fighting for respect. He felt very comfortable telling me that respect is all a man has; if he loses it, his life is not worth living—hence, the justification or cop-out for a lifetime in prison. My question has always been, do you honestly feel you are any closer to respect today than you were when you cussed the principal out in the seventh grade and walked away from school for good? During this so-called honorable, self-imposed hiatus, you chose to disregard the responsibility for the rearing of your children. Where is the respect you owe them? You have had to abstain from a lot of family, community, and civic duties required of you as a man and a citizen, or you have had to at least re-frame and redesign them in a manner whereby they fit with your frame of reference, regardless of how they squared with the concerns of others.

The other issue just as impregnable as getting respect seems to be, who must give respect first? For instance, if I am "the man" and you do not recognize that, then you have disrespected me; therefore, I owe you no respect, or I owe you disrespect. This is reminiscent of the chicken and the egg. To my knowledge, the issue of which came first is still being argued.

I propose a solution. If it is not a solution, maybe it can be viewed as a stalemate. Kissing your sister is preferable to fighting your cousins (war). Doesn't the United States still have a stalemate with Korea stemming from the Korean War? I propose that respect has nothing to do with anything exterior to you. Respect must emanate from within. Either you are about respect or you are not. Everything you do or say must represent respect, which is not dependent on anybody or anything exterior to you. When your respect is derived from someone or something outside of you, your respect is open to the whim and capriciousness of any and all forces capable of bearing force on that external object. Your respect is now based on the condition and quality of that object, which means you must prepare to adjust to the respect afforded you, or you must prepare to be disrespected. People's attitudes and feelings change all the time. And we know things change. So to leverage your respect on such flimsy factors or to condition your respect in that manner forces one to settle for conditional respect or to attempt to demand a more appropriate respect when the respect afforded is perceived as inadequate.

If one chooses to demand respect with a gun in the hand, then that respect is coerced respect, which amounts to another form of conditional respect. It is conditioned on the believability of a follow-through on an imminent threat and its duration because once the threat passes, the respect goes with it. Trying to get respect from someone or something exterior to ourselves forces us to have to try to get respect from someone who is incapable of providing it, or to attempt to get respect from someone who may be as confused about what constitutes respect as we are. So the back-and-forth misunderstanding prompts disrespect and becomes a situation where no respect is known or possible.

It is like getting blood from a turnip; it is impractical. Getting this type of respect puts one at the apex of the mountain, to be worshiped as a saint or assailed as a target. Either way, there is only one way to go: down. You were born with respect. No one or no thing can give it to you or take it away from you. You cannot be disrespected by anyone. They don't own your respect. You do. They can be rude, obnoxious, and even vicious, which has nothing to do with your respect. It reveals a lot about them and perhaps about how you need to adjust your relationship and proximity as it concerns you and them. If they say your mama is a whore or slut, whatever your mama is or isn't will remain unchanged by the words emanating from their mouths. All you can get from that exchange is an opportunity to copy rudeness or ignorance.

If you are about speaking and acknowledging others, then do that. Your position is not predicated on the speaking or acknowledgment from others, and it is not time limited. You never allow a negative to define a policy change for what you have already determined to be positive and what best represents the respect in you. Respect cannot be found in the courthouse, poorhouse, outhouse, jailhouse, penthouse, White House, or any other house other than the one God gave you. To look anywhere else for it is to disrespect your Maker.

# Just An Observation

As I was leaving work one afternoon, I noticed a huge gathering at a nearby convenience store. I patiently watched patron after patron carrying various kinds and amounts of alcoholic beverages in a neighborhood that would probably be considered impoverished. My mind reverted back to an incident I heard earlier on the news about a meth lab explosion occurring less than six miles from where I worked. As I tried to connect these two incidents, I thought about how we as a society tend to talk about "children gone wild" and yet neither of these incidents involved children.

Have we grown immune, or have we reclassified normalcy for adults? Is this a sign of what is to be expected in adulthood? Are incidents such as these too minuscule to warrant attention given the nature and magnitude of competing incidents? When I study these incidents in their singular form, I might agree with the former statement. When I review similar incidents and multiply them by the thousands of times they occur throughout this nation and the world, it makes me wonder if we look at these things in isolation for our own sanity. This single incident becomes even more mentally taxing when I think about the fact that most of these adults are probably parents of children who we are quick to ridicule.

Does anyone care whether adults have gone wild? Surely others see the same things I see. Are the professionals already working on these issues making any progress, or are we losing ground? To what degree are these professionals embroiled in similar or greater issues of their own? What's the big deal? Problems of some kind and type and at some level as these have existed since the beginning of time. Most action is futile and is often met with resistance, so why bother? Why not just press on and enjoy life, as they seem to be enjoying theirs? What is the cost? Is the cost too high, and who is really paying the cost? These are certainly interesting observations to me. Has the towel been thrown, or is the fat lady winding down her warm-up? Is this really an observation worthy of more than just observation?

# Childhood Dreams: Bringing a Stick to a Gunfight

My father was an avid hunter, and every Thanksgiving was a special day of hunting for him. He and about three or four old friends from out of state who we saw once a year would come to town for an all-day hunting event. We would often gather around when he came back to hear how some poor unfortunate rabbit or squirrel met its last day on this earth. It also seems I would always hear about the ones that got away from his buddies.

Pop was a World War II veteran, and he often bragged about his experience as a marksman. I could not argue against this claim because every now and then, my father would shoot a snake out of the loft just from seeing the white of its eyes. Other times, he would enforce a no-fly zone above his house by knocking a few birds out of the sky. I don't know if that was legal, but I am pretty sure the statute of limitations has expired or, at the least, I can't be held liable for the sins of my father on this one.

Nonetheless, my father was proud of his guns and kept them on full display in an open-faced homemade gun rack in the family room, or smoke-room, as most of the siblings preferred to refer to it. He dared anyone to touch his guns. He would often schedule a gun cleaning or a hawk blade filing on my sisters' dates, just to introduce their boyfriends to the close vicinity of his weapons of mass destruction and the expediency with which they would be employed from his household. My sisters would still be virgins if I had to date one of them.

One of my baby sister Linda's dates was met at the door by my father one night after a gun cleaning and given the riot act because of his late arrival—10 p.m. My father thought he should have had better sense not to come at 10 p.m. because he had to leave by 11 p.m. I never saw that fellow at the house again.

But my father's love and fascination with guns is probably what made my first experience so memorable . . . and almost so deadly. I guess I was about five years old when my brothers Gerone and Lenwood and I were playing cowboys and Indians, a popular childhood game at the time. Seeing how we could not afford the latest weaponry, my brother Lenwood and I probably had a stick for a gun. Somehow my brother Gerone had no intention of losing, so he was the only one with a real gun and live ammunition. In the final showdown, he had Lenwood trapped, forcing him to raise his arms to surrender, but apparently Gerone wasn't allowing any surrenders and he shot him anyway. The bullet went through one of the hands Lenwood had up and pierced the side of his face. It threw the whole family into panic mode.

The nearest hospital was about fifteen miles away and there was no automobile in our yard, the yards across the road, or a yard as far as we could see. My oldest sister Julia was about as far from being a track star as anyone in the family, but suddenly she acquired track shoes and ran at least a mile nonstop, in a thunderstorm, to Mr. McCrae's house, not knowing if he was home but praying he was because there was no telling where the next vehicle might be. During this time, we could stay home all day and perhaps only two vehicles would pass our house. There were very few blacks at that time who owned automobiles, and the whites whose farms we worked on were not very keen on allowing blacks to ride in their cars. In this particular case, my brother was bleeding, and all bets were off that he would get in one of those automobiles without a tourniquet (on his neck) to stop the bleeding, even though he was a future field hand. Maybe he would have been allowed in the back of the truck that was used to carry farm animals if a family member would lie under him to catch the blood and keep it off the bed of the truck.

These were tough times, and it was tough for the whole family, but we made it through this crisis. Mr. McCrae was home and was able to get Lenwood to the hospital where he was treated. My brother is doing fine today, but he remembers that incident better than I do, especially how hot that lead was that went through his hand and grazed his face. As for my brother Gerone, his memory of the incident is intact, but due to a health incident, his short-term memory is not as good.

This was also my first introduction to "I am my brother's keeper" because in the aftermath of this incident, my father tore through the house like a madman and beat everything that had a temperature. Really, the family pets were not spared. To this day, I do not understand why my dog had to get his ass kicked. Our collective inability, lack of insight/vision, or use of a crystal ball to prevent this brought his wrath on even those who were out in the field putting in tobacco when it happened.

My second experience with a gun occurred when I was about ten years old. I was with my brother Lenwood again, and we were hanging out near a small community store when the owner asked us to help him unload some items. As payment, he promised to allow us to choose something we wanted from his store. As we were trying to make our selections for our labor, we were suddenly confronted by the owner with a pistol in our face, telling us to leave his store immediately before we got shot for stealing. We left those items and some tracks in the store, and I don't think we ever went near his store again. We had been told that this storekeeper was unstable and to stay away from his store, so for that reason I don't think my parents ever found out about this incident.

My third experience with a gun occurred while playing basketball in our backyard, as we would often do in the neighborhood. My brother James stood about 6'6". He towered over most of the guys in our neighborhood. He did not play very much, but on this particular afternoon, he decided to insert himself in the game by using his ball. He often referred to himself as Lew Alcindor, the former name for Kareem Abdul-Jabbar. Well, James got the ball down low where he wanted it, and as he posted up the 5'7" guard Melvin (okay, I am giving him a couple of inches), James decided he would punish him a little by giving him a taste of his treacherous sky hook.

As it looked to me, his hook came in a little low and Melvin put it in the cornfield, or maybe cotton—either way, it went away from the playing area. Well, the whole yard went crazy because the renowned sky hook that no one could get had just been taken out of the park by perhaps the shortest guy on the court. I admit, I usually backed my brother, but it was nasty, and all I could say was he sent the sky hook skyward. It seems everyone was laughing and rolling on the ground in delight. So James took his ball and went inside. This happened to be the only ball we had at the time, but the laughing continued on the court as if they were going to memorialize the spot where history was made.

After about ten minutes, James emerged from the house toting a shotgun. The crowd immediately dispersed and the laughing came to a screeching halt. Nathaniel was generally one of the calmest and smoothest guys in our neighborhood on and off the court, and he was a local hero of mine. So as this incident unfolded, I watched him to get some cues on what to do, but he broke camp. Everyone seemed to panic and was scrambling for a hiding place in an open yard. Since James could not chase everyone, he chose to go after Marvin, probably the ringleader of the laughter.

He chased Marvin to the corner of the barn where I think Marvin alluded to my brother not having any bullets in the gun and unwilling to do anything with it. In short order, James let off a round in the ground near his feet. The flying dust got everyone's attention, and Marvin immediately changed his tune. By this time, there definitely was no more laughter, and the mood had shifted to somber. Calls went out begging my brother to think about the seriousness of his actions and whether it was worth it. As my brother settled down and retreated to the house, Marvin and the rest of the crew left our yard, and I never heard any more talk about Melvin's exploits that day.

You can see my three early experiences with guns were not very good, so I never developed the same love and appreciation that my father had for them.

# Teacher's Pet

I must have been feeling lucky one morning because for some strange, unknown reason I thought it was a good idea to retrieve my fourth-grade teacher Ms. Hicks' yardstick from her designated place and use it for a little amusement. I started to smack the desk of unsuspecting students, just to wake them up or make them more alert if they were already awake. To be honest, I really did not care whether they were awake, sleep, or sick; I felt like playing so my classmates became my playthings.

Everything was going as planned until the classmate in charge, Judy, decided she would put my name on the board. After an unsuccessful bid to get her to remove my name, I advised her that I did not care; she could keep my name on her raggedy board. I even let Judy know that when I was in charge (as if that day would ever come), her name would be the first name I was putting on the board. When the teacher returned, my punishment was to stand in front of the class with my little legs straddling the yardstick. I don't know how long she intended to keep me in that position, but I thought my bobbing and weaving should have signaled that I had enough. Instead, Ms. Hicks went on with her class without paying any attention to me.

When she finally decided I had learned my lesson and motioned for me to return to my seat, I had to use both my hands to bring my legs back under me. My initial walk was a little wide legged and unsteady. After that ordeal, teachers had a difficult time getting me to use a yardstick as a pointer on a board assignment. I guess it is time for me to give up on getting Judy back for putting my name on the board or blaming her for me being childless.

# Head Sister in Charge (HSIC)

Things occasionally got out of hand with young, playful siblings. On this particular occasion while jostling with my sister Mary, things turned serious, and then ugly, as a fight broke out. Well, of course, I got the better of her and started to puff my little chest out as her tears f lowed. By the time my oldest sister Julia arrived, I was still a little warm under the collar. She commenced to hollering and snatching at me, perhaps because I was the oldest and a male. I thought she should have been trying to find out whose fault it was because I was ready to tell her it was Mary's fault. Mary probably stated it as my fault. I felt I was defending myself and since she started it, she got what she deserved. Then, I started thinking it must be stick-up-for-girl-day, so Big Sis must want some of me, too. Furthermore, I barely worked up a sweat getting the preliminaries out of the way so I was ready for the main event.

I then did something very uncharacteristic of all my sisters and brothers: I pulled away from Big Sis and squared off for a fight. I must have caught a sniff of foolishness in the air. I certainly was not ready to move up in class, especially not her class. She beat me like a runaway slave and left me on the floor crying, "Just wait until I get big; I am going to get you for this." That promise is still empty over forty-five years later, but it remains as an example of a lesson learned that did not come from the classroom.

# Bee Encounter

One warm summer evening, my brother James was supervising and helping Lenwood and me gather some dry wood that would be used to start a fire for the upcoming winter months. Somehow James, a.k.a. P-Body, dislodged a hornet's nest, and as he got in motion he neglected to tell us there was an infestation nearby. Lenwood was the first to get popped, and by the time the bees swarmed around him, I believe P-Body, who was already about 6'4" at the time, had his entire body stretched out and was about an eighth of a mile down the road.

For a second, I thought maybe I should act like a rodeo clown and run in and distract the bees. Then I immediately came to my senses and figured the best thing I could do was to get out of my brother's way as he tried to part ways with the bees. So I got moving in the opposite direction while keeping an eye out for the whereabouts of any stray bees. I was prepared for "fight or flight." Don't get me wrong, I wasn't above "screaming like a girl" if I thought it would scare the bees away.

When I looked back over my shoulders, I saw Lenwood performing a very difficult task; he was using all fours to negotiate a ditch while at the same time using two of the same fours to swat the bees. When he hit the shoulder of the road, his feet were fully engaged. Now, I don't know the top flying speed of bees, but I can assure you it is not as fast as a little boy motivated by a few stings. I could see the bees in pursuit but they were unable to close the gap. When he reached the house about a quarter of a mile down the road, he went airborne onto the porch and into the house, leaving those bees in his wake. As for James, well, I believe he had consumed a glass of tea and was preparing to tell his version of the incident for the second time.

Looking back in life, I've determined that my brother's speed was no fluke as I recall him showing up once at an integrated track meet with a pair of three-inch disco platform shoes and a little alcohol in him and humiliating the second-fastest guy on our track team. I was no slow leak but I needed a pair of Adidas Supernova Glide 3s and a serious tailwind just to finish neck-and-neck with the fourth-fastest person on our team. When the coach asked me to get him, I wanted to tell him, "Isn't one embarrassed guy enough for today?" Instead, I dropped my head and told him I needed to take a shower.

# Toys Are Us

Growing up, I never had the problem that many children experience today of tripping over toys or not being able to get in their room because of the toys. Toys were a luxury that not only could we not afford, we also knew we could not afford them and knew not to even ask for any, especially in my early childhood.

In the absence of toys, I got creative. I would stack two bricks on top of each other (the bottom brick extended) to make a school bus, and push it around in the yard. June bugs were the closest I could get to a toy with an engine. I would catch them with a net or knock them out of the sky with a board just hard enough to stun them. Then I would tie a thread behind the hard casing on their backs and extend the string and allow them to fly in a circular motion. Manipulating my tug on the string would create a spiral effect and a change in the sound of the bug.

This was one of my favorite childhood games, and I was sure the June bugs were enjoying it just as much as I was. Besides, they got to participate in my controlled f lying exercise, which is something they would never do on their own. Never mind they got wacked in the head so the games could begin. I can't remember if I set them free after using them as toys, or if I kept them trapped somewhere to use another day so I wouldn't have to knock another one crazy the next day just to get my play on.

The other thing I did for fun was to trap lightning bugs and use them as my night toys. My first experience in this game ended tragically when the lights went out unexpectedly because I didn't know I needed to provide air holes. There are not many things more beautiful than a jar full of lightning bugs on a dark night with no stars.

# Too Close to Call

Maybe everyone has a few uncommon, unexplainable phenomena or occurrences in their life. Well, here are mine. W hen I was about seven years old, I had a soda bottle top, the kind with the jaggy edge, twirling around in my mouth. It slipped down my throat. All I could remember is suddenly I could not make a sound. I could hear quite well, and as I reached for my throat, I could hear my mother directing my siblings to get some bread and water, I guess in an attempt to flush the cap down. The things they were trying to stuff down my throat were not working. I remember starting to feel weak and a little unsteady, and one of the last commands I heard came from my oldest sister Julia was, "Come here, boy." As I used my last little strength to move in her direction, she hit me on my back between my shoulder blades with such velocity that I almost fell to the floor. It dislodged the cap, throwing it and the corn bread and water up against the wall. This was certainly a defining moment in my life that my sister barely remembers.

I found out later she learned this procedure in one of her health classes. They were teaching the back blows at that time as a part of CPR, which was replaced later by the Heimlich maneuver. As living proof of its effectiveness, I would not discourage the use of it today, especially if one did not know anything else. I also tell kids to pay attention in class; you never know when you may hear something that could save your life or the life of someone else.

I am not good at auto repair work or anything with my hands, unlike my brother Lenwood, so I am not sure why I was attempting auto work without my brother's input. I must have figured my brother-in-law, David Earl, would be good so we were working under a car at my father's house in Maxton while my father watched.

We had the car jacked up with a pair of blocks under it for added safety. We worked under the car for about thirty minutes, pulling and yanking on things. We needed a tool that we did not have, and even though one of us could have gotten it, we both got out from under the car, figuring this might be a good time to take a break. As we were walking away from the car in the direction of the house I heard a thump. I looked back and the car we had been under no more than ten seconds ago fell flat to the ground. I looked at my brother-in-law, and he looked dazed.

All that night I kept telling myself that was divine intervention at work. What a difference ten seconds can make!

One night my father and I were coming home from Fayetteville on Highway 401 south. There was an approaching vehicle in the left lane when suddenly, out of nowhere, there appeared a vehicle attempting to pass the vehicle coming toward me. I thought to myself, "He knows he can't make it. Surely he is going to slow down and get back behind the vehicle he's attempting to pass." Instead, I heard him punch it; it sounded like one of those old four-barrel carburetors had just opened up, and I knew he was coming fast and furious. It was dark and raining, and we were all traveling above sixty miles per hour with blinding lights and not much of a shoulder to steer on. Exiting on the shoulders at these speeds and under these conditions was very tricky and risky, but I remembered from Driver's Ed that any collision is better than a head-on collision.

As the vehicles moved toward each other, it was as if I had some help steering my vehicle onto the shoulder. Almost instantaneously, the original vehicle I was facing also veered onto the opposite shoulder, and the maniac kept his vehicle straight, and all three vehicles passed safely at the same time. Now, if you are thinking that the occurrence of these three miraculous incidents are evidence that God's presence is off-and-on, just read "Footprints in the Sand."

# Information Age

Information is not neutral, and it is not innocent. Those saddled with the dissemination of information do so with a purpose and an agenda. Most who are affected by that dissemination are clueless as to the craftiness and efficiency to which information has been delivered for centuries. Once information is seasoned and properly packaged, its digestion is a matter of when, how much, and how often. When information with the right flavor is consumed in the right quantity, the consumer thereafter becomes a willing participant and advocate, and may even become a little indignant if the information feed is interrupted by a competing interest purporting a dupe. What to believe and who to believe becomes a high-stakes game where the economics of winning become more important than the validity and reliability of the information.

It is hard to imagine where we would be without information. It is also difficult to fathom life separate from information, yet they are separate and have always been separate as far as the ability of one to exist without the other. So why should the neutrality of information matter? If one is unaware of the effects of information being presented, one becomes vulnerable to them. When the masses are unaware, the effect—whether positive or negative—is multiplied in such a grand manner that it should never be viewed as innocent. The lack of or existence of information has saved, extended, and destroyed lives. Likewise, information or the lack thereof has produced millionaires and created paupers, sometimes from those same millionaires it created. Life and information have somehow become one.

Where and when information and life merged is unclear, but the merging is undeniable. Once engulfed in the continuous and seemingly endless process, the prompts are clear, saying, "Stay tuned, the information age is fresh and tantalizing." It is also addictive. The consumers are the new addicts, non-diagnosable and, therefore, ineligible for treatment or service. Never mind, part of this new condition's challenge is denial, slipped in with the innocence of the information. The consumers are now helpless, bankrupt of awareness, allies in their own alienation, but very useful to the specific agendas of the information disseminators. This has been going on for centuries. Knowing the value of the economics of the future, can we really depend on the information disseminators of yesterday to promote an agenda inclusive of others' agendas if it is counter to their agenda? It would be like Ford sponsoring Chevy's ESPN Clubhouse's commercials.

As I attempt to lay out an argument to be mindful of information, affected information bodies may counter with a warning about my agenda; to them, your ignorance may be bliss. A coin toss on whose agenda should prevail is weighted against me. My status as an irregular player in the information dissemination arena may get me lambasted as a crackpot or a player hater. Often when professionals deliver information it has been sanitized, flavored, and presented with an appearance of innocence and usefulness to the consumer. It may have several uses; however, one, some, or none may be useful to the consumer. It is always useful to the disseminator. There is very little reason to suspect or inspect information for anything other than information; herein lies the hope of the disseminators and the vulnerability of those being presented.

Because information is without boundaries, it affects the old, young, poor, rich, kind, and angry alike. A two-year-old child who can barely pronounce her favor of one restaurant over another may be viewed as funny, trivial, and insignificant by the parents, yet to the disseminators of the information responsible for insinuating that choice into the child, this is very significant and valuable market data to be studied and rolled into the dissemination of future information. This is the science of predictability. If the parent believes and thinks the child's behavior is only worth a good laugh, then the actions and behaviors of the parents serve the interest of the information disseminators as well. Don't think the data on the parents isn't just as important as the information on the child. Yes, information is too powerful to ever be thought of as innocent or neutral. As a conduit to the hearts and minds of millions, it has been at the base of all histories; it is part of a seemingly innocent continuum, and it will be at the end of all destinies.

I am not advocating that information is good, bad, or indifferent. I am not implying transgression or corruption with the dissemination of information, nor am I saying there need to be new disseminators of information. My effort is to encourage a deeper and broader thinking, understanding, and consciousness about the interest, flow, purpose, and significance of even a morsel of information. In information, as with all things, the wholesale welcoming and acceptance of newness (all things unknown) in the blind is dangerous. At a minimum, if not received with an appropriate measure of temperance, it can be tricky and slippery. Fickleness and gullibility are two words commonly associated with the unsuspecting public. They are also the same two words most useful to the information disseminators. Consumers, be aware.

# Uncommon Rats

We had to be creative in the country to keep a watch out for fun because we never knew where it would come from, and sometimes our fun was rather strange.

One thing I used to do for fun was to observe and try to predict when our household pets were going to demonstrate they were willing to earn their keep. When it came to the cats, I guess their natural inclination was to chase mice and rats and, of course, devour them when they caught up with them. Well, as it turned out, we had some of the largest rats I had ever seen in my life living beneath our feed barn. The cats would squat and wait near a rat hole and pounce on the first thing that came near the exit. Sometimes a cat would find itself in a fight with a rodent that outweighed it and which was fiercer than the cat.

I don't know how sharp our cats were, but I could tell immediately when a cat was in over its head and a little shocked by the fight in the meal it was trying to obtain just by the effort the cat was putting in trying to get away. After a tussle at a rat hole went bad for a cat, I would make a game of it by monitoring and observing the cat for a week or two to see if it would return to the hole. I was unable to pinpoint any predictability associated with a cat's memory or nature. What I was able to gleam was that my childhood history books were right because cats seem to love to prey on mice and rats. Sometimes they would find themselves a nice meal for their patience, and on other occasions, they would find themselves in a fight for their lives. I must say the scraps were fun to watch. It was like watching The Nature Channel without the narrator. The action was always fast and furious. Who needs pay-per-view and 3-D when I could step out the back of my kitchen and witness a brawl so classic that it would rewrite history when it culminated in a rat chasing a cat?

# Stealing Gas

One late evening, my brother Lenwood, two friends Curtis and Bobby, and I stopped in at a neighborhood store to get some gas on our way to our favorite partying spot, "the Dead End." Everything seemed fine until the next morning. My father stopped by the same grocery store on his way to church and the grocer advised him that he recognized two of his children as the ones who stole ten dollars of gas from his store the night before. My father was less than a mile from the church and about two miles from home, and I am pretty sure he had ten dollars from our work in the fields to pay the man.

Now, my father drove everywhere without a license, thus, one would think there would be no need for any unnecessary risk. Why not just pay the man, get your blessings, and let us get some extra sleep? Not my father. I imagine he almost blew a gasket just from listening to what his sons did. I wasn't in the vehicle with him as he left the store, but judging from the manner in which he charged the house, I doubt he drove the speed limit. Thank God it wasn't mating season for the deer.

At that time I slept on the top bunk and Lenwood on the bottom. Normally, a person just can't wake all at once from a deep sleep, but when one is hurled out of the top bunk onto the floor while getting drenched with saliva all over my droopy eyes, I had no other choice but to gather some wits about myself rather quickly. While my father was grabbing and shaking me, I think Lenwood bumped his head on the top bunk trying to stand up. I believe we both took about two minutes of steady back-and-forth abuse before we finally figured out what he was talking about. Lenwood questioned me about whether I paid the man, and I questioned him, but somehow in our haste to get to the party, we neglected to pay the storekeeper.

Once my father stopped shaking and shouting, he instructed both of us to go immediately to the store and pay the grocer, apologize, ask him to forgive us, and volunteer as servants if he needed us to do anything for him that day. I did not think it took two people to pay one person ten dollars, so I was thinking rocks, paper, and scissors. Of course, I didn't mention anything that could be mistaken as a weapon while my father was irate. I did think that maybe luck would be on my side this time and I could get back into bed since I was the one awakened by a real nightmare of being thrown from the top bunk. Neither of us asked my father if one of us could stay back while the other went to pay the storekeeper. My father returned to church. I hope he went to the altar and asked forgiveness for his treatment of us. On second thought, I'd prefer he stayed away because all he probably would do is ask for more strength to get hold of us some more.

# Got Milk?

My cousin John a.k.a. Skitter lived with us for about three years. He was about two years my junior and was a restless little fellow, seemingly always looking for some mischief and keeping all of us in some kind of trouble. When he was younger, he thought my baby sisters were just for his amusement, so he would shake the house down just to get beat up by them.

One evening my father asked me to go to the store, about two miles from the house, to get some milk for my niece Jo. John wanted to tag along, and I agreed to the worrisome company. We got to the store and got the milk and everything was going along just fine until John said, "Let's swing by Mr. Douglas' house," where Cynthia, Marilyn, and Mary Lou lived. At first I said, "No, we got what we came for, let's go home. It's almost dark, so what do you think you are going to see?" John countered with, "It's less than half a mile away, so what is it going to hurt? Uncle Gary would not even know the difference."

Well, if the truth was known, I could use a glance or two at Marilyn. I am not sure whom my cousin John wanted to take a peep at, probably even the mother if she had veered within his sights.

As I got near the Douglas' house, I was preparing to turn into the driveway to turn around but had to wait for an approaching vehicle. As I waited for the vehicle to pass, I noticed a fast-moving vehicle coming up behind me, and I heard the brakes slam and then screeching tires. Before I could make my turn, I was rocketed forward as he slammed into the back of my truck. The driver staggered out of the car, claiming his brakes had failed him, and I was just stunned. I had never been in an accident and did not know what to do. Wonder Cousin was standing there looking like a blind frog on a foggy night.

All I was thinking was that I didn't need the cops or my father and what in the world was I going to do. I thought I needed to kick my cousin's ass and then have someone—other than my father (he was a professional ass kicker)—kick mine for listening to him. Before we could exchange names, another car coming at a pretty high speed crashed into the vehicle that hit me, so now it was beginning to look like a small pileup in front of the Douglas' house. I recognized that driver as Mr. Christian, and I thought that before he recognized me as Gary Calhoun's son, I had better leave. Yes, I left the scene of an accident. I had seen enough and figured that the driver who hit me had gotten what was coming to him, and I might as well go figure out what to do and go get what's coming to me.

I really was not in a rush to face my father, so my cousin and I drove around trying to think of something to tell Daddy about why it took us so long to bring the milk. Maybe we could tell him the store was closed or did not have any milk and we had to go to Laurinburg, about fifteen miles away, to get the milk. Well, because of the amount of time we took, we surely needed an excellent explanation, and I was running out of even bad ones. There was no way he would believe that the whole town of Laurinburg was out of milk, so we had to go farther than Laurinburg just to get milk.

I even thought we should just keep driving and never come back. We had already initiated a fast for the baby, and if we didn't get home soon, the milk was going to be sour. How were we going to explain the big dent in the back of the truck? My cousin tried to argue his case after witnessing how angry I was with him. I quickly told him he needed to tell that nonsense to my daddy and stay as far away from me as the front of the cab would allow because I was beginning to have a meltdown where his safety was concerned. I was thinking that maybe he needed to ride in the back of the truck. Now, this was before the movie "Throw Mama from the Train," but throwing and dismemberment were my immediate thoughts, just in case my father left me in no shape to make good on my thoughts at a later date. I took no responsibility for the trouble I was in. I blamed it all on my cousin and saw no reason to be rational as it related to consequences for him.

I guess my cousin thought he had an inside track to my father's good side, so he volunteered to tell his uncle what happened to his truck

47

and I gladly complied. I certainly did not try to discourage him from that assignment. I used the darkness to shield the damage on the truck and pulled in the yard in a manner that would shield the damaged side and parked it in a way that my father could not easily see the dent. Maybe he would not notice the dent until a few days later; by then, my mind may have cleared enough to figure out something it hadn't figured out thus far.

As we walked up to the house, I saw my father waiting for us and I saw the anger in his eyes and all over his face, even though it was dark and from a distance. My cousin apparently did not pick up on any of those cues because he casually walked right up to my father and started to say something. Before he could get it out, though, my father smacked him so hard upside the head that I ducked and grunted as if I thought it was a two-for-one swing, even though I was at least five feet behind him. As my cousin passed through the door, my father double kicked him in his ass. I thought to myself, "Finally a good ass kicking well deserved." When my turn came, he whacked me upside my head, and I went down and put my butt on the floor. I figured there was no need to make it available to him since I knew from watching my cousin that my daddy was in an ass-kicking mood.

# My First Wheels

I remember the day I noticed a muscle car on a ramp. At the time, this was often how they displayed vehicles for sale at car lots. I thought to myself, "Now *that* vehicle has my name on it!" It was a 1970, beige V8 318ci Plymouth Barracuda. First, I talked to my dad about the purchase, thinking he would be excited for me, especially since I was not asking him for any money. His advice was for me to keep driving his old pickup truck and save my money for college. Although that was not bad advice, I thought it was time that I get my own transportation, probably because his smoking chick magnet was better suited for spraying mosquitoes.

So I ignored his advice and went straight to my aunt Jane, who recently had been robbed (less than two months earlier) of $1,300 after she forced a bank teller to count her out thirteen one hundred dollar bills on the top of the counter. Unknown to her, she was being observed by two opportunists in the bank. They followed her outside and made another withdrawal and relieved her of her every penny, which the police never retrieved. I just knew she would cosign for me, but she said, "No way."

I started to tell her, "You just gave those robbers one hundred dollars more than I need for the entire purchase and I am putting fifty percent down." I also wanted to say, "That's why you shot yourself in the leg. It is the Lord way of trying to get you to be less stingy." I really didn't know anyone else who came close to having what I needed or could help me in the purchase of this car. After two days of trying to convince my aunt I was a good risk, I gave up and took my $600 to the guy who owned the car lot and told him that I tried but I could not find a cosigner for the other half. To my surprise, he said, "Kid, I don't think you want to lose your $600, so I will do something I have never done before. I will sign for you because I believe you are going to do the right thing." Well, I could have kissed him but instead I shook his hand and told him he would not regret it. My payment was $60 per month for twelve months, but after seven months I had repaid my entire balance. I would always remember that a stranger had more trust and faith in me than my aunt, and it was my responsibility to honor that trust and faith with the utmost respect.

# Intelligence

Sometimes I think too much is made of intelligence (IQ) tests, especially when being touted as the measurement that matters the most. An intelligence test that measures the capacity to get along with people seems to be more essential to marriage, parenting, business, and running a country. I read a story once about an employer who searched the world for the greatest chemist. He found him in some faraway land. He had tremendous talents and impeccable skills. The employer entered into a contract for his services, but after a couple of months, he had the whole company in such an upheaval due to his agitation about every slight that the level of productivity went down dramatically. The employer had to let the man go because he just could not work with anyone.

As a middle school counselor, I often mentioned this story to my students. Sometimes it is difficult for students who are a whiz in math and science to understand how something that is not a part of their end-of-grade test would have such a bearing on how far they go in life. "If it is that important," they would ask, "why is it not a part of some of our classroom assignments?" It never seemed to interfere with the awards and honors they received, and it was not a factor in their moving up in grades. A society that measures progress by obtainment of things, assignment of titles, and the swiftness of which both may be obtained might suffer some backlash for putting "getting along with people" ahead of other measures.

The focus on intelligence is often an "I" endeavor, which is counter to the endeavor of "we" or "us" in a "together" exercise. Intelligence without the capacity to transfer it so it can benefit more than the individual with the high IQ is like a library; it is full of intelligence but if you cannot get the knowledge off the shelves and into the hands of those who need it, then the abundance of intelligence or knowledge is useless. The ability to transfer intelligence and engage others in the accomplishment of ideas as well as things is an important component of intelligence.

I was by myself in Germany once in a department store of some kind, and I needed to use the restroom. I could not find anyone who spoke English, and I had made the mistake of waiting until I really needed to use the restroom before I started trying to find one. When I did find what I thought was the restroom, there was no picture sign indicating whether it was for men or women, so I had to wait until someone came out or went in. I mention this not to say that I have a high IQ—but had I had one—that high IQ may have included a sense of superiority, arrogance, and egotism that tends to frown on interacting with others, especially when the "high horse" is saddled with the position of needing assistance as opposed to giving assistance.

An individual with an IQ of 150 who is unable to get along with anyone and who finds himself in an environment where getting along is a must, might appear dumb rather quickly. If that same person is compelled to grapple with life-and-death decisions and he continues to abstain (remain in the clouds) from engaging effectively with others, then that person and his high IQ might perish.

# Hoop Dreams

The camaraderie of the corrections staff contributed to the desire to organize a staff basketball team to play against other correctional facilities in the area and throughout the state. Some of the area institutions' staff were not large enough or did not have enough athletes to have a separate team, so they borrowed from other facilities to make a team as we did on rare occasions.

I was fortunate enough to be chosen as their coach, although almost everyone knew more about organized basketball than I did. Nonetheless, the friendships and time spent together honing those relationships were priceless. Before I get too far, I just want to say what happens in Vegas stays in Vegas, so any such exploits will not be a part of this article.

We had some great guys on our team, and we had a lot of fun traveling to different places. We had famous names like Davis, and famous-sounding names like McArthur. Then there were Mims, Love, Frahn, Maynor, Galbert, Black, Manning, Quick, Womack, McNair, McCallum, Haynes, and perhaps others I am unable to recall or who joined the team after I left. As their coach I don't think I ever got cooperation on my first request: "Could we wait until after the game to get drunk?" What I meant was, "Could we hold off on the celebration until we won?" I don't know, but I thought perhaps it would give us an advantage or edge on some of the other teams that chose to party before the game or maybe we would just be sharper if we were sober. I had no luck with the party animals, so perhaps I had it wrong; maybe they were more fluid and played better because we racked up tournament win after tournament win. I think that over a ten-year period, the Hoke Correctional Institution staff team won or placed in all but three or four of the tournaments we entered. Many of those wins came after my stint with them.

Much of this may not have happened in the manner I am describing had there not been a rule change. In the beginning, we were only allowed to use currently employed corrections staff to make up a team. The participants agreed to allow one non-staff member to be a part of the team. I thought about several people, but Officer Black was convinced he knew the best person to add to our team. His name was George Maynor. I did not know this guy but that soon changed for me and everyone else around the state. In his first outing with us, he dropped about 50. This guy could light it up. I learned later that he was one of the best shooters on the 1979-80 East Carolina University basketball team that set the ECU field goal percentage record at close to 50%, and he was a fourth-round pick of the Chicago Bulls in 1979. Maynor later joined the Hoke Correctional Institution staff. His son Eric is a former member of the NBA's Oklahoma City Thunder.

As for the Hoke Correctional Institution Men's Basketball team, its thunder is pretty much asunder. The Hoke Correctional Men's Basketball team's star was a trail blazer, therefore, it is only proper and fitting that his son would end up in Portland.

# Bike Week or Nike Week

About a year after my divorce, my brothers Wendell and Lenwood came up with the best idea in the world to get me out of what they called my depression. For about as long as I could remember, the Memorial Day weekend appeared to be the culmination of Bike Week in Myrtle Beach, South Carolina. What better medicine than the scenery of an unlimited supply of females in thongs stretched out on the back of motorcycles to bring a man out of his cauldron of despair?

Against my instincts I made this trek, although I was not in complete agreement that I was in a depression or needed this particular therapy. Because it gave me an opportunity to spend some time with my brothers, I agreed. When we arrived at Myrtle Beach, the place was abuzz with all of what my brothers promised. It was definitely a festive atmosphere and from what I could see, there was not a lot of social inhibition. My brother Lenwood was telling me that I could not tell him that I didn't enjoy what I was looking at. When I told him I wasn't blind or dead but that I preferred the company of one woman at the beach, I was accused of not being a man and certainly not a Calhoun man. If he and Wendell were going to think I was girly, at least they could have considered me to be Nike, the Greek goddess of strength, speed, and victory. Wendell was not in complete agreement with Lenwood, but he was definitely leaning more toward his position than he was mine. I could tell that the wheels of their minds not tainted by spirits were still turning. Well, in any case, they had a designated driver, and I still had full control of all my strength, speed, and victory—a Nike.

# Work . . . a Humbling Experience

After my college days, it was time to go back to work. I left the factories in search of more fruitful opportunities, and I told everyone they would never see me again. I found the job market a little tricky. Now that I had my college degree, employers were telling me they were looking for experience. Before I went to college, they said they were looking for a college degree. I had never heard the word "experience" so much until I got out of college. I wanted to work. I contacted my cousin Roy Mack, the army recruiter, for perhaps a career in the military. I talked with him twice and met with him once at his office, but I was not convinced this was the direction I wanted to go in unless I could go in as an officer.

Besides, they did not have a plan where I could take my girlfriend with me for the next 20 years. I was told if I wanted to be an officer, the best time to have pursued that avenue was prior to my junior year in college, which is when I would have taken Basic Training. I still could pursue an officer's route, but it seems I had a lot of work to do to get accepted into Officer Candidate School. I declined, and then made one of the toughest decisions I ever made in my life.

I was always a good worker, and the factory I left vowing I would never return to had an opening. At that time, it was the most viable option for me. I walked back into that factory, and they hired me immediately. For four months I took, "College boy is back; he couldn't stay away, y'all. He is back on the line as a rookie, except this time, boys, he's got more education. Maybe he will load that truck with y'all more intelligently. Maybe we ought to get some college-level ideas on how to make eight hours of production in four hours. Boys, if you all need some help, don't ask the supervisor; ask the college boy. He has four years of advanced studies."

Lastly and mostly, I think, I was told if I got any more bright ideas I just needed to keep them to myself, because I could have saved that money I put in college if I wasn't going to do anything but return to a factory line. For four months, I do not think a day passed that I wasn't ridiculed. The day I left I was very happy. This time, though, I did not say I would never return, and I have not said that about any job I've left since.

# Burning Bridges

I have always heard it's not a good idea to burn your bridges because you never know when you may need that bridge on your return trip. Well, on my next job, you might say I blew the bridge up before I got across, and I think my career stayed in the dungeon as a result of my opening act.

Maybe I was a little too young and dumb to understand diplomacy, but when the top person looked me in the face and said he had no job openings and I handed him a job listing at his agency indicating over fifty openings in the criminal justice field. Each of these openings required an acceptable criminal record and a high school diploma. I also had two relevant degrees beyond high school and did not even have a parking ticket. To say the least, I got a little heated when I could not secure an interview. I told the superintendent I was going to the Department of Corrections headquarters in Raleigh the next day to find out why I was being told there were no openings at a state government facility listing no less than fifty job openings on a state employees posting at the very address where I was being told there were no openings.

"Not that you have to hire me, sir," I said, "but I will ask why I am being blocked from applying to be considered when I clearly have more than the minimum requirements for the job." He tried to sneak in "over qualified" as the reason and that I wouldn't want a job beneath my qualifications. I said I have never seen an overqualified, unemployed guy preferring continued unemployment to underemployment. Which one pays the bills? If that's the case, I'll take two of those jobs. Give me a sergeant slot, maybe even your job, but don't tell me I am overqualified, yet you have no place for me. Being overqualified to me means you get an employee at a bargain; you can't say you did me a favor or you gave me something I didn't qualify for or deserve. He told me there would be no need for me to go to Raleigh and he could not promise me anything, but he needed me to come back the next day and bring my high school diploma.

That must have been my interview because I never interviewed for anything. After a couple of tests, physical and maybe psychological, I was called in about two weeks later to report to work as a corrections officer. The way I came in meant I would never be a favorite son, and I was okay with that. After about four months on the job, I challenged the seniority policy by citing evidence of my request to move from third to second shift being passed over by staff with less time on the job. This really had to do more with me trying to secure more time with my woman than favoring second shift over third shift. She worked second shift at the time, and I figured we could maximize our time with each other if we were both on the same shift.

My complaint finally got to the person in charge of third shift. I was summoned in to see Lt. Hunt. Covering his right and left flank were Sgt. Lunsford and Sgt. Lewis. I immediately sensed this might be a hostile environment and that the two sergeants present for my personnel matter were not my witnesses because they were not there at my request. After I refused to eat the bologna Lt. Hunt was trying to serve me about how much he needed me on third shift and how important my experience was to the department, he gave up, shifted gears, and revealed why he had the two sergeants there in the first place; he pulled rank.

After rearing back and blowing out a puff of smoke from his pipe, he said, "Listen, son, I am tired of jerking around with you. I am the shift commander here, and you will work where I damn well tell you, and if you don't like it, you can let the doorknob hit you where the good Lord split you. Now get the hell out my office."

Years later, I remembered a scene in "Lean on Me" where a desk was flipped over on Principal Joe Clark, played by Morgan Freeman, Jr., and I remembered I had those same thoughts in my situation but instantly aborted them when I reflected on the fact that I had a home loan being processed. I knew that being without a job and having a criminal record for doing what I was thinking about doing would set me back tremendously, and this didn't take into account the ass whooping I was going to take. I could see the write-up placing all the blame on me for my own beat-down, with them being the victims of an officer gone rogue. Further statements might have read that the supervisors, out of fear for their lives, had no other choice but to use all means at their disposal to put me down. Who knows what I would have been sprayed and hit with? Most of my injuries would have been written up as coming from my own hands or as the result of not complying with legal instructions. The supervisors present would have most likely been victims of unprovoked violence, and the record would have reflected that they acted only in self-defense.

A final dagger may have been an assertion that I was in the lieutenant's office without permission when the melee broke out. In fairness, I must say these are all conjectures and are only possible outcomes based on my later knowledge and experience of similar incidences involving staff and inmates at that institution. So I smiled and said, "Thanks for your time. I just needed to know who I was dealing with." I guess from that exchange, my chances of being the lieutenant's favorite son had evaporated also.

When I finally got to second shift, I think something not so good must have followed me because I was consistently assigned to C-4 (a punishment detail) and a position so insignificant that they did away with it altogether shortly after I left the custody department. I could have bear-hugged the air out of Chambers after he selected me for the program department where I fared much better with Jackson, Singletary, Styers, and Beatty, later McQueen by marriage. I finished that transitional part of my career with Minshew, Monroe, Gillis, Mitchell, and Thompson without any of the hiccups I experienced earlier.

# Business as Usual

Ronald Reagan once said the most terrifying words in the English language are, "I'm from the government, and I'm here to help you."

I thought I might share a truth I learned which underscores that sentiment somewhat after my dealings with a few government officials. I don't know how many times I was assured I would get all the help I needed. Well, I am not sure about that, but I did get all I could stand. I will attempt to describe some of my business communications with some of the government officials and policymakers without divulging specifics. You are free to put it in where it fits in your life experiences. Anyone who has spent time dealing with city hall on an important matter may be able to relate to this information. The expectation that those in our government who write and enforce policies are always on the up and up, fair, and will play by the rules has been purged from my thinking. Let me put this out front so those reading this will think I have neither lost my mind nor my faith in the goodness of mankind or the government. I think that having a government that serves its people is a good thing, and I would rather live in a country with a functioning one than in a country where government is nonexistent.

Now, I have heard that our government is involved in espionage—covert, overt, and disinformation of all types—against all foreign and domestic threats to our security, whether they are real or manufactured. In its proper context, I suppose this is prudent. However, for government officials to engage in such tactics against its ordinary citizens as a matter of routine practice came as a shock to me. It created a condition in me that I refer to as Acquired Suspicion Syndrome (ASS). You will not find this condition in the mental health manuals ICD-10-CM or DSM-IV-TR, but for me, it is a real condition. I also know this condition had a recent onset because I did not have it prior to my business dealings with these government officials.

There were times in my communications when I thought they didn't even care that they were wrong. It was like I was dealing with high-level, very clever, well-armed thugs. I really felt as if I was in a no-holds brawl and for me to have any chance at survival, I would need to arm myself with something other than impeccable character and sound and fair business practices. I have to admit I was naïve, and I was caught off guard. As the battle raged, it became very difficult to isolate the good guys from the bad guys. Not everyone was tainted. However, by this stage in the game, I was suffering from ASS and could not tell the difference. I sensed that some inside and outside dealings had been conducted by how far ahead some of my colleagues were in the game. Those government officials not privy to any complicity were genuinely surprised by how some suspected of not being above-board were able to navigate the process with ease despite the tough new policies.

Sometimes I think those who make policies are only good at making policies and know very little about practical application. There are some highly skilled policymakers, and they are very good at what they do, which, I think, is ratcheting up policies to make what they do appear very essential and relevant. They seem to plug policies with a myriad of vital pieces. They subject the policies to constant addendums while mandating real-time compliance from imperfect people and imperfect systems, which will guarantee a level of failure eventually by everyone. What would a policymaker do if everyone was doing every-thing right and the policy was perfect and needed no improvement?

A maze of complexities is a built-in part of the process of constructing a policy and a requirement to making it a good policy. It took me some time to appraise that perhaps this charade was mainly a cover to facilitate the interest of certain players, mainly bigger, well-connected corporations, against the interest of less-connected operations. It was about who should have access to the available dollars and whose criteria and agenda should be used to determine that. Bigger corporations generally have deeper pockets and are better able to quickly facilitate unfunded mandates. They also generally have greater access to high-level political operatives who can elevate their status from consideration to passable. Government workers know they cannot do much about certain big business players (see the too big to fail policy).

Instead, the government operatives will go play tough guy and flex their muscles by enforcing their policies to the letter on the less-connected businessman, putting him in the same helpless position that the big corporate operative puts the government officials in. At the end of the day, the government officials can act like they have done their jobs, but the only person they were able to affect was the less-connected businessman. About the only thing that the government official can say about the well-connected business owner is, "I tried to do my job, but politics got in the way." When it comes to big businessmen and the top-level government officials commingle is standard practice. Conflict of interest exists at every level of our government. It's not a secret, and it's not personal against the less-connected businessman; it's just business.

I think they thought that the extent of my understanding of how it all works should have rested with what the government officials told me, because my queries were always viewed with contempt. Collectively, politicians on both sides of the aisle make concessions, earmarks, and offerings to special constituents or groups and stick all taxpayers with their bill (the law) and that other bill (the cost), while they collect all the benefits of their deals and run off and invest in so-called blind trusts. Allegedly, close to fifty percent of those who leave Congress apply as lobbyists, and others go to work for large corporations using their fresh influence to enrich themselves and their cronies. It's not a conflict; it's just business.

"60 Minutes" ran a piece on Lobbyist Jack Abramoff on November 6, 2011, where he claimed he had sway on at least 100 members of Congress through bribery and influence peddling. I dealt with a culture of arrogance that either suggested the impossibility of any improper influence on their policies or that they were much too intelligent and insulated for me to do anything about their decisions even if there was some impropriety. I know now that these government officials were mostly puffing and engaging in face-saving efforts due to activities orchestrated by others outside the lines and beyond their pay grade.

Every time the government says it is going to clean up something and make it better, it is very successful in adding more paperwork and policies. This usually amounts to increased business expenses in the form of unfunded mandates. The government puts forth information on how much things have improved or will improve. Then the government readjusts the research to reflect stated outcomes and continues with business as usual. It's the American way, or is the way Americans have gone astray? It's deception from its inception. Either way, it is just business . . . as usual.

# A Crushing Love

As I was trying to piece together many of the parts of my life, I found myself deliberately avoiding this section because of the many mixed emotions I knew it would conjure up. Many of these emotions I had longed buried and promised myself I would never revive again.

I met my wife-to-be at what in our neck of the woods we called our country Mardi Gras a.k.a. Picnic or Bluff. The event (usually the second or third week in August) of fun, food, music, and games was literally a place carved out in the woods where almost everyone from our neighborhood and the surrounding neighborhoods gathered each year. In 1972, a little girl caught my eye, but my gait must have been too slow; it would take me a year to finally catch up with her. Somehow I missed her for the rest of that year, although it was not for lack of trying.

Now, we did not have a car in our driveway—excuse me, I mean yard—but generally, we could get a ride to attend the fair at least twice before it would leave. There were actually three of these fairs that came sometime in August: the Bluff, Picnic, and Skillet. The last one was a little farther away, and I can't remember attending it but maybe once in my life, and I do not think many of us knew exactly where it was. On the occasions when my father would leave me some of the money I earned working in the fields, I would use it to find a way to the Picnic or Bluff. My brother-in-law Joe Anderson would always take me and my brother Lenwood and maybe another friend or two if we would pay for the gas and agree to push his car. You see, the GTO he had was a straight drive and seemed to always have a weak battery, so wherever it stopped it had to be pushed to get going again. Of course, we would try to help him find a hill to park his car on to make our task less difficult. Pushing was a small thing, because we would have pushed it to the South Carolina line if it would take us closer to the girls we were trying to see.

I could always tell when I was getting close to the fair by the bright lights and smell of cotton candy, popcorn, and sausage dogs. When it rained, everyone got a bonus in the air, the fragrance of a hog pen and other natural matters. However, the music of James Brown, the Ohio Players, Kool & the Gang, and others always brought with it a feeling that everything was going to be all right. The Ferris wheel and swings had kids hollering in unison while going up and down and round and round. It was our Mardi Gras.

Well, back to the little girl who caught my eye. After a year passed, I knew I had to come up with something better than what I had used in the past—a hope and a prayer—if I was to be successful. I did run into her on a weekday, but there was that friend of hers, whom I later learned was her cousin, Barbara Ann. This presented a problem for me because I needed separation to work my plan. I decided to return that coming Saturday night with a partner. I nabbed my cousin Alfonzo to use in my buddy plan to pick off her cousin if they were traveling in twos again. Alfonso and I set out to survey the terrain and in about fifteen minutes we ran into the two cousins, so I instructed Alfonzo to pick off the cousin and I would clean up the girl who was left.

Well, either Alfonzo was hard of hearing or hearing hardly mattered to him, because he picked off the wrong one. I almost became undignified as I tried to explain to him that I had been trying for two years, counting last year and this one, to catch up with this girl. After regrouping, the plan went off without a hitch. Later that evening I found out Diane had several sisters, Geraldine, Gloria, and Julia, and a niece name Tina, and they all looked similar to each other, leaving me wondering if I had the right girl. The eerie resemblance contributed to one of my nieces; Yolanda, Tameka, or Jarmonica, uttering the statement, "take me to that house where all those Diane's live. Actually, she had four more sisters, but they were older and lived in Baltimore, Maryland.

I found out Diane lived in McColl, South Carolina, which was closer than where I went to school in Maxton, North Carolina. I did get her phone number that night, although I learned later she only gave it to me to get rid of me because she did not think I would use it. Well, when I got the number I had no idea how I was going to use it. You see, we did not have a phone and out-of-state phone calls at the time were very expensive. Nor did I know anyone who trusted me to use his or her phone to make that type of phone call. So, as it turned out, she was right; I didn't call her.

I had lost girlfriends previously because I did not call after I told them I would. I was always too embarrassed to tell a girl I did not have a phone, and when I tried to come straight and explain the reason I did not call was because I could not secure a phone line, I would be called a lying dog and told to stay away or don't ever speak to them again. So by taking this number, I knew there was a good chance that what happened before could happen again, but as it turned out, since she did not think I was going to call her, it worked out as she expected.

After I took almost two years to secure this meeting, my initial presentation was almost derailed, at least in the eyes of my future mother-in-law, Ollie Mae. That night, I sported a nice afro, but when she saw that I wore my hat backward, she advised her daughter against the likes of me, stating that any boy who would wear his hat backward did not know where he was going, and no daughter of hers was going anywhere with him. Without a phone or automobile, I communicated mainly by letters. Sometimes my letters would be so thick that Diane's mother paid the mailman extra to receive them. She advised Diane to tell me that I needed to make my letters thinner or put more postage on them, because she was not going to keep paying for my lies.

My schedule got tight when I started college in Hamlet, North Carolina. I lived in rural Maxton with my parents or in the city of Maxton with my sister Naomi. I worked a full-time second-shift job in a textile mill in McColl, South Carolina, and carried a full-time college load my first two years of college. It was school, job, and home, and each was about twenty-five minutes apart. For two years, my life became a routine that went like this: Up by 5:45 a.m., to do homework or class preparation, at school by 7:30 a.m., leave school by 3:00 p.m. or 3:30 p.m., and at the job by 4:00 p.m. to 12:00 midnight.

I literally would change out of my school clothes and into my work clothes while driving 60 miles per hour on Highway 381 South just to get to work on time. My social life suffered tremendously. On Fridays, I would generally pull a sixteen-hour shift. Because Diane lived in the same town where I worked occasionally, I would swing by her house after midnight to say hello and steal a few kisses. Many times on the weekend I would fall asleep on her shoulder, prompting her to anger or to call me boring. When the choice to continue my education arose, I had to fight the temptation to follow my heart or complete what I had started. We did keep our long-distance relationship intact, and I made it my business to see her as much as possible. She was available on most weekends when I could get home, except on the few occasions when she was gone with her friend Leroy. Oh yeah, and her mother also kept paying for those thick letters I was sending!

At the end of my bachelor's education, I considered entering law school but opted out because marriage was calling. Any youthful aspirations that conflict with the heart will soon lose favor and follow the ways of the heart. Middle school and high school sweetheart-ism is the biggest challenge and threat to academic procurement. Diane and I were married nearly twenty years, and I never had the words to fully explain how much she meant to me. Up until the year of my divorce if you asked me about my greatest accomplishment, I would say it was my marriage. She was the first person to accept me and my stuttering and showed no hint of embarrassment when traveling among her peers. I enjoyed being with her and did not need anything else but her to be happy.

I once thought that if I was given a life sentence and it included her, it would be easier to do that time than it would be to do a week's sentence without her. I considered her my best friend, lover, and confidant. I was faithful to her my entire marriage and prided myself on keeping the females at bay. I only had one rule for all my female friends. "You and I are not ever going to share a secret that I can't tell my wife, for to do so puts you closer to me than my wife."

I will stop to mention one of the most brazen attempts at usurping that rule came in an offer that was packaged as platonic, that we were so cool that we could take a shower together. Well, those who knew Ginnie knew that if I had followed through with that one, my one rule would have been undone and this whole section would be written very differently. Let's just say she must have been Michael Jackson's inspiration behind "P.Y.T.," because every time I hear the song, I think of her. There is certainly more I can talk about, but this one seems to stand out the most.

One of the most difficult and stressful times of our marriage came when we were trying to have a baby. Our doctor explained we had what was called a double whammy, which meant there was a fertility issue with both of us. He advised that endometriosis was a little more common and much more receptive to treatment than my extremely low sperm activity and extremely low sperm count. Therefore, we sought the expertise of a male fertility specialist. It was during this period that I endured some of the most humiliating and embarrassing medical procedures of my life. Procuring and providing sperm samples became a routine procedure. Matters of timing, sperm care, and maintenance made lovemaking more of a textbook ordeal and doctor appointments just another of the ongoing mechanical assessments of the most private and intimate moments of our lives.

This was all being done with expenses outside our medical coverage and the knowledge that the odds of success were not in our favor. We kept enduring with the hope that we would be the ones who cheat probability. Once when I was alone with my doctor, he advised in a frank manner that because of our double whammy our chances of being parents together would be nothing short of a miracle. He also advised that if my wife did not get pregnant soon, there was a good possibility of her endometrioses reoccurring and losing her window of opportunity, perhaps forever. He was basically saying that she would increase her chances of becoming pregnant with someone else and so would I. But, in the fertility business, people beat the odds and surprise the medical profession all the time—well, not all the time, but it happens. "Miracles happen every day," he said, "and it can happen for you also."

In my case personally, he advised I had a much greater chance than my wife of not ever being a parent, and he wanted to know if I could accept that possibility. The second opinion I received was blunter. He stuck with the medical science and said that miracles belong with the immaculate and virginal conception, and perhaps I needed to have that conversation with my priest. It was definitely a hard pill for me to swallow, so I say to those who can have, or have had, children without extra services or procedures, please do not take your blessing for granted.

Most of my twenty years of marriage were blissful, and although it did not end how I would have drawn it up, it was time to move on. It had outlived its usefulness and to continue on our present course would ruin the memory of what was accomplished and probably would leave two people miserable and bitter. Some good things do run their course and when that course is run, it means the running of a new course must begin. I will always love her for sharing a major part of her life with me that fostered an opportunity for both of us to grow and develop without embedded ridicule, shame, or abuse. I still consider her among my friends and would not hesitate to assist her in matters of need as I am able.

The absolute worst feeling in my entire marriage came in a phone call from my wife when she casually asked if I had been dreaming about fish, a myth in some cultures, which means pregnancy, is amiss. Initially, it did not dawn on me what she was trying to say because this was far from my mind. This was a period in our marriage when we had separate living quarters; she had opted to live in one of our rentals, but we were still seeing each other as husband and wife and making love as husband and wife.

My thinking was that she was going through a phase and once it passed, we would continue our marriage. I told her I would never spend a night where she was living and would never make love to her there, and I never did. I fully expected we would get back together in our home as husband and wife and had no idea that, in her mind, she had already moved on. When the news finally sank in, I must say I did think about how we might still make our marriage work with another man's child. I had convinced myself that adoptions are always another man's child and at least this one had one biological parent.

However, after hearing over and over, "Read my lips, I don't want you anymore," my armor of love for her was beginning to crack. It was becoming glaringly clear to me that I had a decision to make. As painful as it was for me personally, it was even more difficult for me to let go. R&B singer/songwriter Usher would explain my situation a year later in "U Got It Bad," but there was no getting around the inevitable, which I had to accept.

Yet, before I actually moved forward with the divorce procedure I couldn't help but subject myself to some more abuse by calling once more to see if she was absolutely clear about the direction we were taking. Then the final straw occurred. She said, "You haven't done it yet." That hit me like a ton of bricks, and for the first time, I felt alone. I had no one I could call who could do anything about it. She did not care to go through the proceedings with me; she just wanted me to get it over with and just let her know when it was done. I was faced with something I did not want and didn't know anything about, but I knew it had to be done.

I had always thought divorces were for other people, so my mind was too far away from that type of thinking to grasp what I was hearing, but from how she was talking, my mind had to catch up fast. When I hung up the phone, I began the longest and loneliest walk of my life; a time I had always prayed and hoped against was upon me and all the faithfulness, love, hard work, and commitment I had used to guard against this ever becoming my fate had failed me. I had to take that walk; it was a crushing love.

# A Leg Up

My father had a few hobbies, but I believe he had one hobby that trumped them all. It was supposed to be a form of discipline, but I use the word "hobby" because he seemed to enjoy it so much. Although he reserved this hobby for the boys, all of my brothers have stories about being kicked around.

Once, my father went outside the home and put his foot to a neighbor and friend Ralph's butt when he caught him skipping school with my brother Gerone. There's no telling what kind of combinations and leg action Gerone got. He would partake in this hobby over something very simple. One day my brother Lenwood and I were playing near the road, and my father—while walking toward the road—yelled for Lenwood to come to him. I don't think we were doing anything wrong, or at least, that was not conveyed to us by my father. There didn't seem to be any urgency in my father's request, so I guess Lenwood was not in a hurry.

Lenwood must have thought this was a good time to demonstrate his pimp walk. He was moving in the direction of my father, but something about my brother's pace or style set my father off. Without saying a word, my father picked up his speed in Lenwood's direction, and I knew immediately he was not hurrying to him to talk. When my father reached my brother, he passed him just enough to get enough room to extend his leg fully, and as it made contact with my brother's rump, he launched into the air. I don't know if this was my father's intention, but when Lenwood came back down, the pimp walk was gone, his gait was back to normal, and his speed had been adjusted upward. My father loved to say, "Get the lead out," after he kicked you, so I guess when Lenwood sped up, it had something to do with the lead being out.

Sometime after that when my brother Gerone was seventeen years old, he explained to me that he had been kicked so much he could not remember what his butt felt like without a foot in it, and he had been

72

thinking it was time to put an end to this ass-kicking around here. I told him he had been listening to too much Rudy Ray Moore. His recommendation was that the brothers should get together and the next time our father kicked one of us, that person should keep his leg going up and put him on the ground or floor and the rest of us should come to our brother's aid. I thought to myself, "Yes, he is going to need some aid, but let's not forget the 'first' part." Gerone had bold aspirations, but I didn't hear him volunteering to be the one to grab my father's leg.

Now, I was thinking, I am a little too young to leave home, or go to that other home, so maybe Gerone needs some additional information before we proceed, and I know just who to get that information from: Daddy. Now, the word "snitch" might come to mind at this point, but I would rather call it satisfying an itch, since my brother seemed a bit shortsighted. I also think the word "snitch" isn't bad when compared to "death," "broke up," or "hospitalized." Less than a month after Gerone suggested mutiny at Gary Calhoun's home, some startling results were revealed: Gerone turned eighteen and became government issued (army) and the only one of my parents' children to skip a senior year of high school. So maybe he had a secondary plan all along to hide out somewhere for a month if his insurrection did not work. I don't think he had a plan for the rest of us, and that is why I think it was wise on my part to seek additional information.

# 307.0

Stuttering is listed in the DSM-IV-TR as 307.0 and is published by the American Psychiatric Association as a disability. Now there is a lot of technical jargon associated with the diagnosis, such as sound and syllable repetitions and sound prolongations, and although the occurrence of only one is needed, all eight of criteria "A" fit me. As for "B," the disturbance in fluency interferes with academic or occupational achievement or with social communication; that applies to me also. And "C," the speech difficulties are in excess of those usually associated with these problems. That's a given.

As a child, all I knew is that people teased me and shunned me like I had a plague due to a condition I neither understood nor wanted. Every time I opened my mouth and it was not for eating, like E. F. Hutton, people listened, but it was only so they could get a good laugh. Growing up was miserable and painful and to mention it to my father was useless, especially since he would not give me the time to get it out. He would always give me the standard statement, "If they pick at you, they are not your friends."

But I wanted friends just like any other boy. I wanted to say, "Sometimes you pick at me. My siblings sometimes tease me. I have even caught teachers laughing at me. None of them are my friends, either, I guess. Will I ever have any friends?" It all hurt and it seemed no one understood or cared very much. Maybe they were preoccupied with their own problems. Many times I just wanted to disappear, although I did not know how or where.

At one point early in school, I made a conscious decision to not speak at all, and I would get a beating for not speaking when the teacher would ask me to respond to a question. I would often know the answer, but speaking made me a target for outright or sly ridicule. The teachers who forbade teasing couldn't catch everything. Kids were cruel and creative; some would mock me by holding their mouths open and gesturing that they were pulling words out of it for me. I concluded I would rather take a whipping than talk. I often joked with my friend Kaye that I did not go to recess because I didn't play, but the truth is I didn't go to recess because I didn't want them playing with me. I can remember a teacher asking me why I did not want to go to recess, and I would put my head down pretending I didn't feel well. Well, sometimes it would work, and sometimes I would get another beating, especially if the teacher did not buy that I was sick.

I was considered for special education once because of my slurred speech and lack of speech. My lack of participation in class work did not negate the fact that I was an above-average student, and that is perhaps what kept me from going into special education. I was somewhat happy one time when I was told I would receive speech therapy. Before the semester was over, I was told they had no more money for the program. All I remember is I worked on the "th" and "ah" sound and thought I was making some progress before it went away never to return. I am sure that the ending of speech therapy did not make me feel I was worth a whole lot. The school district must have had many more projects more worthy of spending its money on than me.

As I got older and I figured not much was going to change, I did become a little more comfortable with myself, and since many of my classmates remained the same, some of them had teased me so much they had grown tired and bored with it and would leave me alone. Little did any of them know I contemplated bringing a gun to school long before the kids who orchestrated Columbine were born, and even though they were fleeting thoughts, all kinds of things ran through the mind when a person is hurting and feels helpless and just wants it all to end. At times I felt cut off from anyone who cared, so the range of emotions that I did not understand was overwhelming and scary. I felt alone, and it was there that I started to sort everything out and began to understand my choices to be imploding or empowering. I am most thankful that I did not follow through on some of my most desperate thoughts.

My anger did subside little by little as I grew and became more interested in girls. It is not that girls were less cruel, but my upbringing about the treatment of females made it more tolerable coming from them, and it disallowed retaliation or anger in a violent or physical manner. My female classmates and schoolmates did not have any problem telling me they were not interested in me and that the reason was because I stuttered. I often joked with Louise, a very good and honored friend today, about how cruel girls were to me. I think now we all understand the sheer cluelessness of being a child. I will list some of the less shameful attacks on my speech follies. Some comments were, "I don't want a country boy and I sho' don't want one who stutters," or "What would I do with a country boy. Hitch him up to a mule and the mule will probably talk better than you?"

I have been told, "I would not go out with you if you were the last person at this school." I often thought even the girls who might have been interested in me were succumbing to peer pressure and would not return my advances because of that. It became a little hard for me to enjoy school because I knew I stuttered, but I kind of felt like I was not a bad person and just did not see why others did not see that. I can see now how going through it all grounded me and made me more amenable to the disabilities, challenges, and woeful conditions of others.

Once in the ninth grade, a new girl came to our school from New York; I later learned that her move to our area was by way of Laurel Hill, Gibson, John's Station, or some small town that would make Maxton look like a metropolis. If I had that information at the time, I could have thought of her more like a homegirl, and been less blinded by the glitz. Anyway, her name was Linda, and I just thought she was the most beautiful girl I had ever laid my eyes on. Maybe this was my chance to get a fresh start with a new girl who didn't know anything about my stuttering. Oh, we had player haters back then, too. But if I thought she was beautiful, I knew that fact did not get away from others, so I figured my stuttering ass didn't stand a chance. Still, I could dream. And dream I did!

When most of the guys would talk about their rap game, I was just happy if I could put two words together without stumbling all over myself. A year later, I talked myself into trying to make a move on Linda, but first I had to come up with a rap. I thought about asking some of the guys known for having a good rap around school, but I didn't want to look stupid or give away why I wanted it. So, I wrote my own rap. I put it on a 2 x 4 card, and I practiced it for two nights. It was very simple. "Hi, my name is Howard. You are very pretty, and would you be my girlfriend?"

On the day I chose to make my debut, Linda was standing beneath fluorescent lights looking like an angel at the entrance of Mr. Thomas's room, her science teacher. I paraded up and down the hall passing her at least three times, greeting her with a nod, trying to get my nerve up to approach her. This actually was my second day at this; the first day I thought about how to initiate the plan for so long the bell rang before I even put my plan in motion. So on this day, on my third walk up and down the hall, I threw caution to the wind. My knees crumbled the closer I got to her. I became so nervous I almost passed out. I opened my mouth, but nothing came out. I begin to stutter like I never had before.

When I finally got something out, I think I told her my name was Linda and that I was pretty; I believe I forgot the rest of the rap. I wanted to go through the concrete. That Southwest Airlines commercial, "Want to get away?" comes to mind. I tried to avoid her for the next two days, although I think I had at least one class with her and skipping class—well, Daddy didn't play that, and I already had enough pain in my life. Anyway, I don't know if my rap would ever worked as I never got it out, and besides, I should have known better because she already had a boyfriend and I knew she would not have dropped him for me.

Linda and I never became a couple, but she did become one of my closest and dearest friends throughout high school and beyond. I don't know if she ever teased me about my stuttering; she could have slipped it in during some of our many lighter moments when I thought she was laughing at my jokes.

I've got countless stories, too numerous to mention, where I tried to hide my speech impediment only to have it expose me. On one occasion during my sophomore year and my very short football career, an older, recently graduated schoolmate dropped by the football field and thought he recognized me. He said, "You are a Calhoun, aren't you?" Then he said, "You are the one who stutters," as I was known in some circles. I started to tell him that it wasn't me, but after I said "it," I got stuck and I said "won't" four or five times, and when it seemed like I could not get off "won't" I needed another hole to get in.

Even an inmate decided he would get in on the act of teasing me after I took him and some of his cellmates to Southern Correctional Institution in Troy, North Carolina, on a basketball outing that we were privy to do at the time. He said, "Mr. Calhoun, we could have won that basketball game if it wasn't for you. I saw you going to the referee and you were saying, *T . . . ti . . . tim . . . t . . . ti . . . tim . . .* and by the time you said, '*timeout*,' time had run out." He may have had a point, but we lost by 30. I straightened him out, and he almost ended up in the hole until I could get "release date" out of my mouth.

On a lighter but related note, a friend, Pandora Tew, whom I worked with at the time, was adding to my stuttering stress level by trying to keep me on the phone well beyond the fifteen seconds I always allotted myself for controlled speech. I was struggling to keep my stuttering under wraps, and I was absolutely terrified of answering a phone or learning that a phone call was for me. She put me in a serious bind because, on the one hand, I felt it unconscionable to hang up on a friend; yet every time I tried to nicely get off the phone, all I could hear was "Wait, let me tell you about this or that." It is amazing how living with a condition that attracts abusers contributed to paranoia, because like a preacher who keeps preaching until he gets a rise from his congregation, my years of being teased and abused prompted me to think Pandora was just trying to keep me on the phone so she could get a cheap laugh on me. I know that not to be the case now, but at the time, I was struggling so badly with my stuttering that I used to pray that she would not call me. Other times when I could not hide in time, I was treating people like they were bill collectors by telling my wife to tell the person I was not home.

In the end, I owe thanks and credit to Pandora's heavy dose of Exposure Therapy as the dominant thrust that propelled me to face my speech demons.

# Simon Said

Early in my criminal justice career I worked as a corrections officer. At that time, orientation was on-the-job training, so I did not have very much to go on as it related to what to do or what was expected of me by way of job duty. I was fresh out of college, and many of the things I was witnessing were unfamiliar with anything I had seen or learned in my textbooks. I had been assigned to B-Block, and one of the first things we did after shift briefing was to report to a designated area. On this particular night on my way to my duty station I walked upstairs to the nurse's station, which was between A-and B-Block. I stopped by the small lockup section across from the nurse's station just to canvas the area. When I stepped into the room, I noticed a senior inmate holding an oversized steak over his eye. Well, I had never seen this before and I thought that this explained why I had never seen any steaks in the dining hall. So I said, "You like yours raw, huh?—No, what's with the steak?" He said it was Officer Simon. He said something about how he needed to change bunks. They spoke back and forth, and the next thing he knew, Officer Simon hit him in the jaw. I was thinking that he didn't appear that clear, so perhaps his age was a factor in how he remembered things. Then I thought maybe it happened so fast that he really couldn't recall where he was hit or who hit him.

I was new on the job and was trying to figure this out without accepting it was who he said it was. I thought to myself, "Now he knows what he mouthed-off about, but he is unclear about what Simon's instructions were to him." Officer Simon was one of the most respected officers by both inmates and staff, and he had a reputation for being fair, which is why I was having such a hard time believing the inmate.

My learning curve was getting ready to take a big dip if Officer Simon hit an old man just because he felt like it. So, I approached Simon, still thinking that the old man had fingered the wrong guy, and I jokingly said, "Didn't your mother teach you to respect your elders?"

He said, "I am still trying to teach him to respect authority. I think he got it now, though." This confused me a little. I was really serious about learning my job and what I needed to do to be a better officer, and here was one of the most admired officers almost nonchalant about knocking an old man out, and then the management staff bypasses the nurse's station and jams as much E. coli as they can in the inmate's eye before slamming him into solitary confinement. I was beginning to feel a little sorry for the old fellow, because somehow, he could have avoided that shiner had he paid attention in recess and just remembered to do what Simon said.

# Fame or Shame

My take on fame is not unlike many others, but when I say something so outlandish that it may be the root of many mental illnesses, I know I need to elaborate and back it up with some research, medical science, or some expert opinion, which in itself is indicative of what I am going to rave against. So this is just my "little ole me" opinion.

I describe fame as the conferring of overrated matters by overrated individuals, bodies, or agencies and reinforced by regular subjects and other overrated mediums. We live in a world where people and things are equal by nature at birth but are suspended to an unequal state through accomplishments and images. This is advanced and expanded throughout life, and although the natural and true states are bared equal again at death, attempts to superimpose the unequal accomplishments and images at death as trump of the norm become the norm.

When I watch ordinary people being carried away on stretchers at a concert and I am criticized for even mentioning the folly of it, I am also being reminded of the normalcy of such behavior and how abnormal I might be. I am told such things as it is just entertainment, and didn't I behave like that at one time. That person will grow out of it; let them have their fun. Besides, there are no documented lingering negative effects associated with such behavior. Well, no, I have never acted like that, and not all the people I have seen act that way are going through some teenage or youthful phase. I have seen such behavior in more than a few seasoned subjects.

As for the documented negative effects, even if that was true, it does not make the existence of negative effects untrue. I heard Oprah Winfrey once comment that people cheered as she returned from a bathroom.

There are so many things that occur in life with family and employers, i.e., roles and titles, that remind people constantly about their worth, value, and self-esteem. These things tend to bind people in a routine of thoughts and views about themselves and their relationship to the world. Mostly, I think we tend to see and identify ourselves in how other people see us. So when we strive to enhance our status, we look for confirmation from those we have identified as somehow more accomplished than ourselves and not those less accomplished. So, if we see ourselves as lowly and others reinforce that perception at home and at work, our mental health is steadily being battered, and we have not even left our community. So, somebody who wants to be anybody but himself but finds himself stuck with what he thinks is nobody is on the road to depression.

When people refer to people as commoners, they are in word and action normalizing an abnormal function of theirs and lamenting an inferior status on what is really a like subject. As the regular guy accepts his lot in life and settles into a life of mediocrity, he fades away beyond the limelight and may conclude that not only does he not matter, nothing he does or says matters. If he becomes an alcoholic or offs himself, what difference will it make to the world? Or he may just pretend to accept his assigned lot in life, develop issues with those or the agencies that attempted to label him mediocre (i.e., Hitler) or diseased, only to resurface with an ax to grind. Other than "Gone Postal," I am fairly sure mental health professionals can find a category for him. Or, he may just decide to collect on his fifteen seconds of fame.

At the other end of the spectrum, those who manage to acquire a high level of notoriety may receive an exaggerated view of how much they really matter. From them, if they are asked, we may hear the issuing of opinions on everything from biotechnology to nuclear fusion. They may have not received a narcissistic diagnosis, but if they have an inability to separate what they do and how the world sees them from who they really are, then they are well on their way to a mental disorder.

I have attempted to explain how the stacking order in a community can wreak havoc on a regular healthy mind; now imagine the number of minds from unhealthy and dysfunctional homes and environments which are already skewed and battered to the point that they just want to assume the identity of anyone or anything other than themselves. Such subjects may be so enticed by the allure of fame that extraterrestrial voices and commands may appear. A split from reality should not be seen as a quantum leap. So-called commoners or regulars are subtly being told to stay in their place or get in step with those who are greater than them. This mental chipping away is also done through various media sources, gatherings, and associations. They soon learn that their value when measured against the value and accomplishments of famous people doesn't measure up, so what follows is a lower view of themselves and a drop of a few notches on the human rating scale. Regular folks are constantly reminded, either up front, indirectly, or by default, to not depend on their decision-making abilities but look to experts for guidance. Rely on the thinking of those who are greater or more important than you.

Years of exposure to such directions and inferences of inferiority certainly will not produce a healthier mind. Now, that's one that the experts and lay people alike can agree on. Behaviors expressing inadequacy, insufficiency, or overvaluation could manifest as pathological and may become chronic clinical conditions. These and more serious issues certainly could be derived from being a part of a local and global environment of values based on delusional and illusionary factors. Attempts at finding a true baseline of self-worth in such a fictitious system contributes greatly to mental anguish and may tender substance use as a viable option. Those who say the world only makes sense to them when they are high are exercising that option. An extreme exercise of that option may very well produce an array of mental health and substance-induced disorders.

Now, imagine CNN running a "breaking news" story that John Doe was just found dead in the Budget Inn hotel. The response would probably be, "Who the hell is John Doe, and why is this program being interrupted?" But if it was John Lennon, it would be accepted graciously and even expected by a host of like subjects who have accepted their unequal and no-count place in life. Of course, the media and other mediums reinforce this as normal, and any break from this thinking is subdued or made out to be disrespectful or not giving this like subject his "unjust" due. It matters little that such idiocy wreaks havoc on all conventional wisdom as well as the mental status of most subjects. A mirage that promises greatness through accomplishments, neutralizes birth and death status, and makes fiction supernatural and reality subnormal victimize us. Is the search and embrace of this pseudo fame a shame, or is it the love and worship of this fame that is a shame and a possible root of many mental health disorders throughout this nation and the world?

# Self-Preservation: The "Big" Question

In the subject of who does the most to destroy this country, the big guy blames the little guy, and the little guy blames the big guy. Now, it is a little unusual that somehow the little guy, who is often synonymous with powerless, is often accused of ruining the powerful. What seems more uncommon about this is how and why the big and powerful would allow the small and powerless to determine a course of anything for them. Even decisions about welfare and other poverty programs are not made or determined by the poor.

Make no mistake about it; all significant decisions are made by the big, rich, and powerful, and they are never made without a benefit for the big, rich, and powerful. Sometimes the small, poor, and powerless can serve as a diversion to matters of interest to the big, rich, and powerful. If something goes wrong with decisions, by virtue of control of the dissemination of information, the blame must go to the small, powerless, and poor unless the big, rich, and powerful would derive more benefit from accepting the blame. The big, rich, and powerful can always rest assured that the employed poor, just by doing their job, will ensure that the poor and powerless stay in their place while the big, rich, and powerful receive any and all brownnosing and red carpet treatment available to them.

For the employed poor, anyone who cannot affect his or her status negatively in any way is someone who does not matter; so even by default the benefit will go to the big, rich, and powerful. This group will never stand idle while a lesser group relieves them of their power and fortune. Even when things go wrong—as they did in the Wall Street debacle and the big, rich, and powerful could not blame the little guy—they blame the system, which, by the way, was set up by them, and when all else fails, they turn to a brotherhood of the powerful to claim a benefit reserved only for the big, rich, and powerful—a bailout. When you say bailout to the poor, it always refers to jail, and it is generally harder to come by than the rich's bailout. What is the most expensive drag on our economy: welfare, or no-bid entitlements and special interest pork? Now, there is absolutely nothing wrong with being big, rich, and powerful unless someone bigger, richer, and more powerful takes the benefit and the former rich and powerful must settle for what the poor, small, and weak always got—a hard way to go.

# Me and Mrs. Jones

While I was in college, this person introduced me to what I called a violent rejection when I asked her out one evening. Perhaps I was a little slow in getting that I had overstepped my boundaries, yet for a moment, I sensed I had desecrated some longstanding custom or violated some unwritten law as she shouted "No-o-o! " She said she was just being friendly.

I think as I slowly backed up, I scanned the room for an escape route and said "Okay." I had already determined in my mind that it wasn't unmanly to run since that was a defense option still available to me. I learned later she was suffering from a Love Jones—the Jones fellow that had her heart, body, mind, and soul, and the one she married less than two months after our conversation. Up until that point, I had never had a person come unglued and unleash her wrath on me simply for asking her out.

Yes, Fatrina, you were the first. I hate to admit that at the time I was broke and could have probably only afforded to take her down the street to Church's Chicken for a chicken and a biscuit and hope that the meal and my conversation would be sufficient. Since she got all worked up by my attempt to secure her as my date, I wondered what she would have said if I had told her that my plans were for it to be a walking date and a Dutch outing. I guess I would have had more than my feelings hurt.

# Missed Education

"My father, who was from a wealthy family and highly educated, a lawyer, Yale and Columbia, walked out with the benefit of a healthy push from my mother, a seventh-grade graduate, who took a typing course and got a secretarial job as fast as she could," said George Weinberg.

I have been told that efficiency in similar education can equip one with skills that can sustain one for life, yet I limped where this was concerned. I had some great teachers, but there were some courses I did not excel in despite their best effort. I will not go so far as to say they wasted their time on me, but it was close. Some things I had a low aptitude for; for others, it may have been a low interest in or a high interest in things unrelated to the subject matter. Hindsight has revealed the most likely culprit for my poor performance was my reasons for taking the courses.

Take Home Economics, for example. Ms. Wesson was very enthusiastic about this subject, and I will explain why I believe it was no reflection on her that I barely made it out of her class. My reasoning for selecting this elective had more to do with aesthetics (wall-to-wall females) than recipes or wardrobe accessories. My performance was a reflection of where my interest lay. One time I sewed up the neck area of a pullover. Unless I was making a Frankenstein or some type of Halloween costume, my fashion statement probably belonged in some other venue. On another occasion, I messed up the orange juice by adding too much water to the concentrated portion due to my nervousness when I learned I was a part of a group assigned to prepare breakfast for the principal.

Typing was another class that promised girls in abundance and my performance stunk. When Ms. Harrell took down her keyboard letters and hand placement poster, I fumbled so badly on that manual typewriter that if I got nine words a minute, it was because Ms. Harrell miscounted an error—and that was about as likely as me making an

A in her class. Besides, outdueling the girls in what at the time were traditionally girls' courses made me ineligible for the help and attention I craved from the opposite sex. Also, being too good promoted the perception that I was more girly than I aspired to be. Maybe that is not all true either, because the next course I did not excel in was supposed to be a man's course, Agriculture and Shop.

My brother Lenwood was a natural in this subject, and consistently exceeded me when he was playing around and I was putting forth my best effort. On the very first day, I remember Mr. Fairley asking if anyone could identify a board stretcher in his shop. My mind immediately went back to the times my behind had been used to stretch a few boards. I thought to myself, living in a house with a few boards missing, I should become proficient in stretching boards just so I can patch up some of the holes in my own house. I knew a thing or two about boards, but before I could get my hand up, my friend Walter volunteered to get the board stretcher for the class. After about fifteen minutes of futility, Walter gave up and confessed to the class that someone moved the board stretcher because he could not find it. To my surprise, Mr. Fairley announced there was no such thing as a board stretcher. I was glad Walter beat me in showcasing his short-comings in matters of Agriculture and Shop, because as it turned out, I would get the whole year to highlight mine. I did not fare very well in this course, and I could not blame this one on girl watching.

As a final thought, Mr. Fairley's motto was "Make me look good, fellas." Well, I was unable to represent with my product, so I tried to make him look good with my effort, attitude, and behavior. In the end, there was some evidence of missed education.

# Kids Will Be Kids . . .

I had a few special childhood friends, Bobby and his brothers, Curtis and Clifton; Walter and his brother, Ralph; and Douglas and sometimes his brother, Frank, and sister, Cathy. We all traveled in a circle between one another's homes and played ball, rough-housed, and sometimes fought. From the greater neighborhood, other guys like Tyrone and his brother Howard, Carnell, and Leon, a.k.a. Hamburger, would come over sometimes to mingle. As I got older, I picked up some friends across the South Carolina state line, such as Larry, Bud, Stick-a-weed, and Johnny.

There are many more, but somehow I recall these as being some-what instrumental in my early development. Kids at that time were shielded from grown folk's business, and the guys talked mostly about females' cute faces and hot bodies. Once while kissing Cynthia with my eyes sort of closed, I thought she sure had some rough lips, and suddenly, I realized her baby sister Ann had jammed her hand between our mouths and was shouting, "Leave my sister alone!" and "Mama, Cynthia got a boyfriend."

On another occasion I recall having such an eagerness and com-mitment to attend school every day only because I did not want to miss a chance of seeing Mary J in her faded jeans or Bernadette J in anything. My guess is that females had their conversations about males, yet as a child, I couldn't imagine myself as anyone's heartthrob. Guys would rush to see female fights, not to pick a winner or loser, but to get a glimpse of a wardrobe malfunction and perhaps seize an opportunity to assist a damsel in distress by helping her reposition a protruding body part or two. Yes, kids will be kids.

In my circle, we did not discuss adult things very much. I think I was aware of some of the misdeeds of adults, but was so immersed in play and teenage silliness that these things did not matter very much. Every now and then I would hear about a grown-up missing work due to drinking or disorderly conduct and needing to be bailed out of jail. Usually the white sharecropper owner who needed the field hand would initiate a release on his word. I do not know how normal or unusual our families and communities were. The adults rarely got into the children's squabbles, and the children did not offer advice on adult matters. As a child, I had my individual battles with my peers. I can truly say I moved into adulthood with a clean slate. I remain friends with my entire boyhood cast today, male and female, if they are still around.

So this is for you, Rodney King, we can all get along.

# Tobacco Row

Being reared in the country had its perks, or was it quirks? I was often told by my classmates and friends that I lived so far out in the country that we had "Whoa" signs instead of stop signs. I had to pack lunch (no dairy products) just to go to the mailbox. We also had tobacco rows so long that they had curve signs in them. The latter part of the last statement is partly true. Some of the rows were so long that I could not see from one end to the other, so they probably should have had curves signs in them, but maybe the Department of Transportation got lost after running a couple of "Whoa" signs.

Perhaps it was not all bad. Since we started working in the fields at an early age, it gave us a jump on driving years before Driver's Ed, although what we drove was a Farmall Super A-1 tractor. I think the overseers were able to exploit our overzealous desire to drive by allowing us to drive the tractor. This meant the bosses did not have to employ another field hand as a driver. It also meant the fieldworkers had to work out an equitable way to move the tractor up and down the field. Rather than rotate the driving equally among all who wanted to drive, the older and faster field hands set up a procedure that favored their speed and experience. The younger and slower croppers had to cheat by not taking all the required leaves off in order to beat a better and more experienced cropper to the tractor seat. We would literally race to get an opportunity to drive the tractor, and sometimes push each other to the ground when two or more would reach the driver's seat at about the same time.

Ralph was one of the more experienced field hands, and he also engaged in a little cheating, so it became very difficult to drive when he was in rare form. It became necessary to teach Ralph a little about sharing, and I was in on the teaching. He loved to pull off by popping the clutch and making the tractor jump and speed down the field to the next stop. On one occasion while he was bent over with his butt in the air and head down to gather as many tobacco leaves as he could as fast as he could so he could beat everybody to the driver's seat, we turned the tractor's front wheels as far to the right as they would go. Just as expected, Ralph beat everyone to the driver's seat, and this time, he took off even faster than usual. But because of the way the wheels were turned, instead of traveling down the drag row, the row designed for the tractor and trailer that gathered and carried the tobacco through the field and to the tobacco barn, he went across three or four rows of tobacco with such velocity that the back and forth and up and down jerking motion almost threw him off the tractor. It accomplished two things: It scared him pretty good and put someone else in the driver's seat. When he got back to his row from getting the tractor back to where it was supposed to be, we were all rolling in laughter while he was still trying to get control of his faculties.

Now, it seems there were other rules that needed to be reviewed, and all of them seem to favor the better and more experienced field hands. It is a little bit like how some rules in society are set up; those who generally make the rules make them to favor themselves or their kind. This next rule, I was told, was designed to increase production. The one who finished cropping his row last would get his butt kicked by the one who finished first or by whoever that person designated to do the butt kicking. Well, it wasn't enough that I was getting my butt kicked at home, now I got to come to the field and get my butt kicked. Being one of the younger field hands at the time, I got my share of butt kicking. They must have gotten bored with kicking the same butts because that rule did not last very long.

My brother Gerone, a very fast cropper, gave the underdogs our first victory once when he used his extra time to sit near the gas tank at the top of the tractor, not realizing he was soaking his pants in gasoline. Part of cropping tobacco meant he kept his butt bent over and pointed in the air, and the unabated rays from the sun heated the gasoline and caused a burning sensation that required constant attention to his rear end. Since there was no place to change his clothes and nothing to change into, my brother was relegated to fanning his behind with a tobacco leaf and rubbing it in the sand, which slowed him down considerably. This took one of the best croppers out of the running as a tractor driver, and since Ralph almost broke his neck, I found myself able to drive a little more than usual on tobacco row.

# Hey, Little Walter

Normally, guys do not do a lot of slumming at each other's house, but when I was in junior college, my friend Walter, who I hadn't seen for some time, came to spend the night with me. I was glad he came; I enjoyed his company, so that was not an issue. What was disconcerting was that he felt getting into bed with me butt naked was not a problem. I immediately alerted him that this was not going to work. He mouthed back that this was how he sleeps all the time and the only way he could get a comfortable night's sleep.

Well, since it was my house I was more concerned about me being comfortable. He said, "Boy, you know I ain't thinking about you." Now, I knew Walter, and I knew he meant everything he was saying, but I couldn't stop thinking about him. I said to myself, "People have had tumors removed in shorter anesthetic periods than the hours required for a night of sleep." So, in my mind, there would be hours to spare for any number of things to happen. I also knew that a man sometimes has automatic anatomy changes overnight and, not to mention, if he sleeps wild and all over the bed, there could be some inadvertent intermingling. I reminded Walter that I had never fought a naked man, but that I was not opposed to it. My thinking was there was no need to risk a good and long-term friendship over a few threads. I told Walter he had to clothe-up or hit the floor, because he was not getting in bed with me like he was born.

# Indecent Proposal

My first job outside the fields was in the dishwasher area of St. Andrews Presbyterian College, which is currently St. Andrews University in Laurinburg, North Carolina. Mr. Hugh, the head supervisor, was a grey-haired, well-mannered gentleman. On one occasion, he told me he was new in town and wondered if I would show him around. I said, "Sure, when?" He said sometime after work. I asked how I was going to get home, which was about fifteen miles away. He said he would take me home, and I was okay with that. He came back later and asked me if I was okay with seeing a movie before he took me home. Again, I said sure, but I didn't have any money for a movie. He said he would handle that. Mr. Hugh came back again and told me nothing was playing at the theater that was worth seeing, but he had an idea about a drive-in movie and he asked if I had been to one before. I said, "No," but that I had always been curious about those shows and would love to go. He said, "Great, then it's settled." He said he would be back and maybe he could get me out a little early. Of course, I was fine with the getting out early.

We went by his hotel, and he offered me a beer. I did not like the taste of beer but just to be grown-up, I took it and started drinking. He told me it would be alright if I brought it with me. Now, I was already too young to be working on his job without a permit, so what's one more rule to break? I was also too young to go to an X-rated movie, but Mr. Hugh said he had that covered. In one night, this man allowed me to break more rules than my father had allowed me my entire life. I was just going along for the fun, feeling more like a grown-up every minute—besides, I was with the big boss—what could be wrong about that?

They must have known him at the drive-in because we just drove in without any questions. The movie as I recall was pretty good. It didn't just jump into a sex scene. There was actually some meaningful conversation. Mr. Hugh threw his hand around the back of the seat, which did not bother me the least; I thought he was just relaxing. A little later his hand moved to my shoulders, so I sort of nudged it off, and he did not protest. Still later, he rested his hand on my thigh and moved it slowly toward my inner thigh. I thought I was imagining things and I was a little slow, but the inappropriateness was beginning to creep into my mind.

I had always been taught to obey and respect adults so nothing about my upbringing had prepared me for this kind of behavior in a seasoned adult, especially a highly respected business owner. I immediately said, "Why can't you stay on your side of the car and keep your hands to yourself?" He said, "I guess I am a little fidgety. Don't mind me, I will be all right."

By that time I was getting a picture that wasn't on the screen, and I was beginning to lose interest in what was on the screen. I said, "Sir, you are a little more than a little fidgety. There is something wrong with you, and you need to take me home or I will walk." He said, "Wait, I am a little bit homosexual, but I am not the aggressive type. I am not going to hurt you." I tried to act unafraid and a little tough with some bass in my voice, so I said, "I know you are not going to hurt me." He said, "Wait, can we just talk before we go? I don't want the wrong things to get back to work." I was nervous and stuttering, but I knew he understood "take me home."

He started to give me an education on homosexuality, explaining that there were two types of homosexuals, aggressive and nonaggressive. First of all, I did not know much about what he was talking about and did not care how many types of homosexuals there were. Besides, I could not get past his first statement that he was a little bit homosexual. I had never heard that before. I was thinking if this man didn't take me home, he might end up a little bit dead. He started telling me that ten percent of the population is gay and that the percentage is probably higher among males because they suppress their tendency more than females. He said homosexuality is normal and that a lot of men have their first sexual experience with a man. I was thinking to myself, "This man is not who I thought he was so I don't want to make him any crazier," but I had heard about all I needed to hear about homosexuality. I thought to myself that I needed to get out of there, so I started to get out of the car although I had no idea where I was going.

He begged me to get back in and said he would take me home. Then he said, "I will give you twenty-five dollars if you let me play with it a little bit." I was so startled that I froze and said, "Are you crazy?" He went up to fifty dollars and then one hundred dollars as his final offer. By that time, I think I was crying and cursing in a stuttering language, but I was demanding that he take me home at once before I ran and told somebody what he was trying to do. I was beginning to lose it a little with my anger and do not remember all the things I yelled, but I do recall telling him he did not have enough money to get me to let him do anything to me. He finally settled back in his seat and said, "All right, you don't need to say any more. I am going to take you home."

I did not want to talk about anything on the way home. I was so upset and embarrassed by the whole ordeal that I never talked about it for years. On the way home, Mr. Hugh said he understood that I did not want to talk, but he wanted me to just listen because he needed me to understand his situation and honor a few requests from him so that certain things would not get back to work the wrong way. He said that if I listened carefully and did certain things, it could be of tremendous benefit to me. Mr. Hugh asked me to promise not to tell anyone at work, home, or the community about anything that happened that night. If I did that, I was advised I could work as I please and did not have to take orders or instructions from any of the other bosses except him. I did take him up on that last offer. When I was late, I dared anyone to say anything to me.

Mr. Hugh must have told the other bosses that I was his personal assistant or not to bother me because, after that incident, all the other bosses were okay with anything I did. I could say, "I am not coming in tomorrow, and I am not going to be sick." In fact, I could say, "I don't know why I am not coming in and only God knows when I am coming in tomorrow." The other bosses would just say it was all right. I must confess I did renege on that other promise not to tell anyone. I did not offer any details, but I told everyone I knew at work that if Mr. Hugh asked them to go anywhere with him, tell him no. As for him being new in town and needing me to show him around, when he took me home that night not only did he not ask me for any directions, he knew where I lived, which was about fifteen miles beyond where we worked. He was not supposed to know anything about the work area so he certainly should not have known anything about the rural area where I lived, which was a different town.

Mr. Hugh was always professional and about business on the job. I believe I worked with him another year and he always treated me as well as he treated the other staff, and he never mentioned anything about the incident to me again.

# Things That Make You Go Hmm . . .

I have had the privilege of working in law enforcement, the prison system, probation and parole (court system), and the public school system as a schoolteacher and school counselor. My experiences have helped me understand firsthand the correlation between incarceration and education. I often mention that prison is for anyone who runs afoul of the law, and I have witnessed doctors, policemen, lawyers, corrections officers, teachers, college administrators and students, an astronaut, and even a state representative behind bars. However, the vast majority of inmates I interacted with every day did not complete high school, and many scored at sixth grade or below on their prison entrance academic assessment test.

I would often tell them that if you increase your education, you decrease your percentage of ending up in prison. As I would review their records, I would find a multitude of convictions and charges listed as priors. I would ask them, "How many of these crimes did you commit when you were sober?" If you decrease your alcohol and other drug consumption, you increase your percentage of staying out of prison. Going against the percentages and betting on the underdog make for good Hollywood endings, but when it comes to freedom, what millions have fought and died for, it is just a clear example of an exercise in poor planning and poor judgment.

Once I thought I could jolt a student into understanding the sheer senselessness of his behavior by explaining that if he insisted on continuing to get bitten by the same dog, he forced me to conclude that he either liked getting bitten by the dog or he was dumber than the dog. He went home and told his mother that I called him a dumb dog, and she believed it. When I explained the scenario to his mother, she advised me that she understood how her son missed the point. I wanted to tell her that it must be a neighborhood dog, but I didn't want to have to explain it to the grandmother, so I just said, "Hmmm."

In another situation, I was letting a child have it about how her behavior in the classroom was well beneath her capabilities and our expectations when she stopped me in midstream by saying, "Mr. Calhoun, if you don't mind, I am going to ask my mother if she will let you just beat me because I can't take all this talking." I must say I never expected that from this student, and it temporarily threw me for a loop. Then, I said, "I am a counselor by nature and profession but I am not fully convinced that a well-administered whopping wouldn't be useful. Talk to your mom. I think I can do them both, at the same time."

# Drunk on the Job

Working in the dish room at St. Andrews Presbyterian College had its perks. High school guys got to look and holler at college girls, and by the first week, most of us had our girlfriends picked out, although the requirement to let them know they had a dish boy was renounced.

One time they had a banquet where wine was served. Three or four of the guys decided to do their part to honor the integrity of the winery business by providing storage space in their stomachs for the unused wine that was being loaded on the conveyer belt. They said it was un-American to waste good wine by pouring it down the sink. There was a steady flow of wine in various amounts being left on the trays, and in less than twenty minutes, those great American high school students were unintelligible, missing a few steps, and holding on to each other for dear life. I am not sure, but I believe they were legally drunk. Reaction time was noticeably impaired and efficiency in work fell sharply. I bet you didn't know that the winery business was in trouble in the mid-seventies. Now you know how the winery business was saved.

# Before the Glory Days

As a sophomore in school, I was trying to learn a little about organized football for the first time. We had a large community garden, a wood-burning stove, and plenty of fowls and hogs so my father had many uses for helping a kid burn off energy. Chasing a football was not one of them. After pressing and begging, he finally agreed to let me play, but he said if I got hurt once my career was over. What kind of condition is that for a contact sport? Had I told the coach that, he probably would not have allowed me to try out. I thought to myself (under my breath, of course) that my father hadn't ever played football. A person could get hurt carrying water or even going to take a seat on the bench. I have seen guys injured keeping stats on the sidelines. It was a take-it-or-leave-it proposition, so I took it.

I got to play in a few games, all the time afraid and worrying I was going to get hurt. I know now that trying to play the game of football while worrying about getting hurt is probably the fastest way to *get* hurt. In one game against Reds Springs, we were getting mauled. The score was 45–0 at halftime. As we gathered under the goalpost, I remember Coach Vaughn shouting, "Forty-five damn points to nothing! My grandma can play better ball than that." And, of course, someone— I think Jimmy Dean—said, "Go get your grandma." Next thing I knew, he had us running around that field like we were conducting a séance to his grandma, and all I was thinking was, "Lord don't let me get hurt running laps because it would be such a shameful way to tell my grand-kids how my football career ended."

I can say, with grace, I got by. I got to stick around a little longer. I saw Allen get his arm broken. Then there was Terry, breaking his leg after trying to stop a McDougald running play, and this was in practice. People were getting hurt so I knew it could happen. Actually, I always knew it could happen; I just wondered why my father did not know it.

When my father heard about Allen's injury, one of the guys from our Piney Grove community, he asked me if I had anything to tell him and I told him, "No, I can't remember how he got hurt."

About a week later my luck ran out in practice when I had to be helped to the sidelines with a pair of cracked ribs. Since it hurt me to even breathe, I knew it would be hard to hide it from my father, but I was going to try. I believe the McColl South Carolina game was coming up, and I wanted to be there even if I had to hobble. When I went home that night, I did my best to stay out of my father's way, but he ran up on me in the kitchen and noticed I was moving gingerly. He asked me what was wrong and I told him I was tired so I tried to sit down and even that gave me away. When he asked me to stand, I asked if I could just rest some more. He said, "Boy, get up from that chair and run over here where I am." I thought I could just suck it up but all systems failed me and I collapsed in pain. He reminded me of our deal and when I tried to act like Franklin D. Roosevelt and proposed a New Deal, I got a blank look, raised eyebrow, and a Howie Mandel "No Deal." It was back to the farm for me.

Maxton High School went 0–10 that season but turned it around to 10–0 the following three seasons (regular season) with the culmination of a state championship, 86–8, over North Duplin. That score still reigns as the largest one-sided championship game in state history. I guess I can tell this as a footnote: In that championship season, I gave my future brother-in-law, Skipper, 35 points for a twenty-dollar bet on a game against second place Rowland High School. When he arrived to the game at the end of the first quarter, Rowland was behind 32–0. He accused me of point shaving or just downright cheating. I said, "You never know what might happen, Maxton might not score any more the entire game, but in case I am wrong, you got my twenty." The final score was 76–0. At the time, I had no idea that this team would average nearly 62 points per game that season. I guess I could have given him 35 more points. I'll text him and tell him he can have them.

# Punk-a-Phobia

. . . the fear of being labeled a punk. I coined that term after a few years of working as a middle school guidance counselor when I kept hearing, "Mr. Calhoun, I am not a punk." Then I shuddered when I heard some of the reasons for making that statement. A couple of reasons were that he looked at me wrong or he thinks I am a punk. On the latter part of the statement, I asked a student once how he arrived at that conclusion. My thinking was, if he and his friends are adept enough to read minds, let's transfer that to academic excellence. I was told, "You know when someone thinks you are a punk, you just know." I would say, "Think, give me the details, and give me the facts."

Then there were the things they would do to prove they were not punks. These things would defy preschool logic. They might initiate a fight on such simple things as a "wrong look" when they knew a fight warranted an automatic ten-day suspension. If they believed an authority figure, such as a teacher or principal, was trying to punk them by directing them to pick up a piece of paper that they claim they did not throw down, they were willing to accept a two-to three-day suspension for a matter that could have been resolved in two to three seconds. Compliance on such matters meant they were a punk and that is unacceptable to individuals in the grip of punk-a-phobia. Many times I thought to myself, "Why not just pick up the freaking paper so the world can get back to spinning?"

Punk-a-phobia was so real and prevalent among these middle school students that it crossed genders. Once a female student initiated a need for a 911 call by turning on a female friend because she believed she was being punked by her friend when her friend donned a jacket on a wintery morning that belonged to a guy she considered her boyfriend. When I questioned her about her antics, which drew the attention and involvement of various factions and nearly produced a riotous situation, she responded by saying, "She tried to punk me."

On another occasion, I was told by a student who ordinarily used many different routes from school to home depending on where he planned to stop on the way home, and who usually traveled with a couple of friends, that he chose to use the exact route a student dared him to take, and he ditched his friends because that same student challenged him to come alone. Needless to say, he ended up in the hospital, but upon returning to school, he was beaming with his wounds, as if the wounds were a badge of honor and respectability. He said, "I told you I was not a punk." So I said to him being called a punk is much more serious than being called a dropout. When I asked if he wanted "I am not a punk" on his tombstone, he said that would be just fine.

As I pondered and probed, I posed the scenario that if grizzlies could talk and they advised they would be waiting for you on the path you just got your butt whooped on, would you take that path again? His answer was, "They wouldn't punk me either, but I would bring my piece for them." He reiterated, "I am nobody's punk and as much as I respect you, Mr. Calhoun, I would not let you punk me either." My standard answer was, "I have an interest in teaching you more appropriate ways to interact to get your needs met."

I think some of the students are doing a pretty good job of punking themselves. Are you one of those students? I have likened this craziness to one of the required features of substance dependency because it parallels it; specifically, the continuation of a behavior despite knowledge of having a persistent or recurrent physical or psychological problem that is likely to have been caused or exacerbated by the substance. So it is with punk-a-phobia. Students who are suffering from this condition are willing to continue in this vein despite overwhelming evidence of the problems associated with this condition. If you are experiencing some of these issues with your teenager, he may be suffering from punk-a-phobia. This appears to be a condition most prevalent in the youth, so the good news is that if he lives long enough he may outgrow this condition; if not, you don't have to spend a lot time trying to figure out what to put on his tombstone.

# Grudges

I think there must be such a thing as a Professional Grudge Association (PGA). Those who belong are an elite group of grudge holders. They possess extraordinary skills in maintaining that feeling of enviousness or resentment over the littlest things for the longest time. Once a grudge is initiated—usually due to a perceived, imaginary, or real slight or injustice—it becomes pointless to issue an apology, because even if it is accepted, it is conditioned with the understanding that membership on the grudge list is permanent, until death do us part; that is, if the professional is without offspring.

Now, of course, humans can say and do some cruel and rude things to each other that may warrant more than a raised eyebrow to communicate dissatisfaction with the act. How one asserts a position and makes that assertion fit and remains consistent with the act without asserting that the person is a villain or idiot will go a long way in limiting the number of idiots and villains who get attached to that one act. Some refuse to talk or communicate with each other unless it is to display their continued annoyance with an act or behavior, even if it occurred two years ago. Grudgers tend to treat people the way people treat them. Their lack of communication will be attributed to other people's lack of communication, and not a choice on their part.

"Why should I speak to her?" she may ask. "She has not parted her lips to speak to me all day, even though I have passed her four times in the hall." Sounds like no one is doing any "parting" and everyone is doing some "passing," but the only "parting" and "passing" that counts is that of the other person. Treating others as they treat you or at least how you believe they are treating you takes you off your compass on how to treat people because so much of how you treat others is now predicated on the actions and behaviors of others. Years of adjusting your behavior, meeting fire with fire, and copying the negative examples of others in response to others provides you with a new routine of behavior that will likely be out of harmony with who you are or who you were created to be. If you did not like the behaviors in the person you are now holding a grudge against, it is highly unlikely you will like those behaviors in you.

In a sense, your biting and sampling of all the negative behaviors that came your way helped you become a compilation of all that you digested. As time passed, you became so much of those individuals you have come in contact with that you don't know who you are anymore. Those observing you believe you are someone to emulate because they believe you are someone who doesn't take any crap off anyone. So, you and your scenarios are spurning a bunch of copycats who will all lose their way. The number of knuckleheads a person will run into in a lifetime is staggering, so just by living one's life, it is not difficult to see how grudgers end up despising what they become. Now I begrudge the fact that the PGA and all its chartered members are holding a grudge against me for my early-morning birth.

# The War of the Sexes

How true is this statement? Men think of a woman first as a sex object, second as a sexy object, and third as an object of sex. The upbringing and conditioning of a man determines the level of truth in that statement for each man. If women are not brought up to share an understanding of that statement, then one can see how men could be from Pluto and women from Mercury.

I have tested the above statement as a theory on a few of my male friends by asking them to share about a particular woman and, without exception, they convoluted my statement by referring to her as an object and offering her physical attributes as a summation of what I asked without thinking about it any further. The women I used in this exercise never used handsome and bulky body parts as their summation. The women talked more about faithfulness, honesty, strength, dependability, whether or not the man was employed, and lastly, good-looking. Women who constantly deal with this rigid pursuit or exploitation tend to suffer from issues themselves by not having the capacity to understand the rationale for the existence of a different pursuit. That first statement, unfortunately, is applicable to many men, but it is not germane to every man. For many, it has become a burden that both males and females have had to bear.

On certain occasions when women have wrongly accused me about my designs for them, I have tried to use the situation as a reachable moment to help them address their EMS, "Every Man Syndrome"—every man treating them as a sex object. As a nonsubscriber, my effort has always been to offer assistance without further contributing to their AARP (Acquired Anger & Rage Personality). For the most part, women generally appreciate and welcome the acknowledgment of their sexiness, usually in the manner, in the amount, and from the person(s) at the time of their choosing. A man who fails to recognize those conditions and boundaries may experience some conflict.

Now, these conditions and boundaries are not fixed, so they could be mobile, vague, and vary from woman to woman. A man's misunderstanding of this is not an acceptable reason for noncompliance. Furthermore, a man who may be viewed as "in there" may fall out of favor, prompting a rule change, which may mean that a rule that was generally inapplicable to him now applies, and perhaps with harsher terms. Falling back in favor may constitute only partial reinstatement. It is recommended and strongly encouraged that the man check with the decider (the woman) more than once before he proceeds as if it is business as usual.

Let me conclude by saying I am not sure about any of this. From where I sit, it looks like there is no end in sight to the war of the sexes. Besides, it's a woman's prerogative, and, of course, Bobby Brown's, to do what they want to do. I still have a few more relationship books to read.

# From Girl²Woman

There are those with whom I can recall my first meeting as vividly as if it was yesterday. Then there are others who have played a more significant role in my life, but I just cannot recall that first meeting.

In 1982, while taking an innocent stroll with my wife around my neighborhood in Southern Pines, North Carolina, I caught a glimpse of a teenage girl, perhaps thirteen or fourteen, carrying a tennis racket. We were fairly new in the neighborhood, so the conversation was more of a general introduction type. Her name was Kym, the daughter of Bob and Lucille, and she lived across the street. She had two younger siblings, Tanya and Kevin. Her household would become a favorite hangout for food, fun, and music. Her beautiful voice and love of music would top off some of the gatherings. I used to go to church just to hear her sing. Maybe I should rephrase that, especially since I was a Trustee Board member for the church. If I heard she was on the program to sing, it would incentivize my being there.

In 2004, she released her CD, The Pain, The Love, and The Spirit, by Kym Verbal, so now I get to hear her as often as I want. As for her tennis game, carrying the tennis racket like a pro made for a memorable first meeting, but I don't think the Williams sisters were ever in any danger of having their accomplishments smeared.

# Business 101

It seems I have heard a lot of things about what not to do in business, but not very much about what to do. "Stay away from family members" appeared to be the first rule I ignored. "Don't go in business with a person who may be a little too friendly with the bottle"—let's just say I am aware of that rule.

My first business was a buying and leasing residential real estate company (Calhoun and Calhoun Real Estate and Investments) with my brother Lenwood as my partner. My criteria for a business associate has more to do with the individual's work ethic, knowledge, capability, commitment level, and the degree of honesty and integrity than a birth order or level of kinship. My brother is certainly committed and has to cover much more than half of the responsibilities in Calhoun and Calhoun Real Estate and Investment because of my ties and involvement in other endeavors. So, in this venture, I am the one who dropped the ball on him more than I wanted or he deserved. My brother Lenwood is very good at what he does and has handled the affairs of Calhoun and Calhoun Real Estate with dedication and diligence. Also, in my brother's case, he has a steady backbone in his wife Sindy, which certainly shores up his résumé as a business partner.

A footnote to this little entry arose when Senator John McCain, during the 2008 presidential campaign, was hassled for not knowing where all his real estate was; I had to break off my chuckling when I realized I did not know where all of my properties were, either.

# Business 102

I have heard so many horror stories about businesses and business partners that I once concluded that the best solution to that problem was to not have a partner, period. So I was very hesitant about partnering with anyone when it came to my next venture. I met my first potential partner, Wanda, in the mid-'90s when she and I had jury duty and she was an alternate juror in Carthage, North Carolina. She offered me an employment opportunity with a behavioral health company she managed at the time. Her experience, passion, and trustworthiness made her the most appropriate choice as a partner in a behavior health pursuit. Our changes in employment and residence eventually soured that opportunity. After several meetings, she chose a different path, and I began to look elsewhere for a partner.

At the time I was engaged in many of these discussions I was working with another friend, Pandora Tew, who, at the time, had mental health rehabilitation experience and later worked briefly with Wanda at Specialized Services. As time passed and our friendship grew, I did think of her as a potential business partner, but never seriously broached it with her because of her military liaison. I didn't know how long she would stick around. One of my most important criterions for a business partner was, and is, ample time to get to know and learn about those enduring qualities I mentioned earlier, and you certainly must have the time and be available. They say when one door closes another one opens, and almost literarily as Pandora walked out, Paula Fleming, my eventual business partner, walked in, all the way from Wimbledon, England. Before I go further with the business discussion, I would like to briefly touch on my thoughts when I first met her. My first thought was that she was beautiful, but that had little to do with my overall views. My beliefs were the result of my southern immersion and lack of acculturation in response to her missing British accent and her African American look.

I should also mention that my way of making new people welcome is to make them a little uncomfortable. I know it sounds raunchy, but I have found that it generally loosens them up to a more fluid disposition and prepares them for a smoother transition into their new endeavor and environment. People have to be uncomfortable in order to seek comfort. When she said she was from England, I thought, "What part of England has a southern accent?" Then she said neither of her parents was military; I said, "Perhaps your parents fought in the South." I decided to really shake her up by telling her that part of her occupational assignment was that she had to take her lunch with me, every day, unless I said otherwise. Of course, she balked, but like a true redcoat, she eventually surrendered.

I learned she had extensive mental health and substance abuse experience dating back to her years in the military. I also found her to be organized, knowledgeable, earnest, caring, honest, and compassionate. That was enough, but as a bonus, she was blessed with seemingly unlimited energy and an unmatched work ethic. Paula has a love of family and loyalty to friends that is almost unheard of in her generation. I am very proud and fortunate to have her as a true friend and supporter in life and a partner at Family First Support Center (FFSC). She is also the catalyst who initiated our effort to return to graduate school at Webster University in Myrtle Beach, South Carolina.

FFSC is a mental health and substance abuse behavior health care agency, headquartered in Mt. Olive, North Carolina, and a part of the Eastpointe MCO catchment area with offices in the Sandhills Center and Alliance Behavioral Healthcare service areas. I am blessed immensely by being surrounded with a tremendous staff of associates. Lucas, Vernetta, Charles, Jeanette, Ella, Perry, Hewitt, Karmashia, Lashaundon, Stringfield, Darden, Truzy and Lee Ray have earned franchise tags for longevity. Cox, Kornegay, Mojica, and Stanley are among the steady newcomers. They and many others are my family and partners in our effort to provide quality mental health and substance abuse service in North Carolina.

# Business 103

I added another partner in executive director Kaye Brimmage to my latest and perhaps toughest business venture, TESS of North Carolina (Taking Education Skills Seriously), a non-profit 501(c)(3) education and social development organization, named in honor of my mother, Tessie Calhoun. Kaye is a tireless, orderly, passionate, imaginative, kind, humble, and thoughtful individual who embodies all the aforementioned qualities with added technology and computer skills that are indispensable in preparing our children for the twenty-first century. She is a trusted friend and confidante, and someone I enjoy spending time with as well as sharing ideas and conversation. I can always depend on Kaye to challenge my thoughts and ideas for growth potential.

We believe that childhood is but for one reason: preparation for adulthood. A child who enters adulthood who did not make very good use of that period, for whatever reason, is an unprepared adult, or put another way, an adult dressed up with no place to go. The doors of childhood have closed on him, and he does not have the keys to open the doors to adulthood nor the skills to navigate the challenges or to take advantage of the opportunities that await him in adulthood. Yet, this is where he is, and this is the place he will spend the remainder of his life. Standing still and/or floundering are options with catastrophic consequences.

My partners and I strive to address this calamitous situation and are reaching out to all who care enough to commit the energies and resources to help make childhood the building block it should be. To date, we have committed close to $100,000 in scholarship money in the form of higher education awards to TESS scholars.

TESS of North Carolina purchased a Rosenwald school in Princeton, North Carolina, in 2008. In the early 1900s, Booker T. Washington and Julius Rosenwald, then president of Sears, partnered in an effort to address illiteracy and unpreparedness in the African American community throughout the South. From 1913 to 1932, the Rosenwald school construction program built 4,977 new schools from Maryland to Texas and many other complementary structures to close a humanity gap created mainly by the policies of the Jim Crow era. Because of the mostly agriculture-based economy of that period, Washington and Rosenwald stressed vocational curriculum combined with basic literacy and numeracy skills. Although this curriculum seems antiquated today, it was relevant and purposeful for the times. Yet, despite the influx of billions of dollars and the benefit of generations of experience, our children are less prepared for the rigors of adulthood today than they were in the 1920s.

Many of our kids are standing still in the gap between childhood and adulthood, and they are getting run over. Some are standing in that gap due to self-induced afflictions and addictions. Others are casualties of systemic overplay and marginalization by our leaders or their policies. It is a misstep for all of us who choose to stand still looking at those who are standing still and in need of our counsel. Generations are being lost. Can we afford, with our inaction, to chance humanity following?

The school that TESS of North Carolina is in possession of is one of tremendous significance and historic value. It once represented a conduit to prosperous adulthood for many. The partners of TESS of North Carolina understand that the challenges are enormous, but we also understand that the rewards are lifesaving and endless.

As I close the chapter on Business 103, this is my most significant venture thus far in my life. I conclude by stating that an investment in our youth is an investment in all of us, for it is the destination of the least of us that will say the most about the best of us. Your inquiry and assistance in the Princeton school rejuvenation project will represent a game-changing opportunity and experience for generations to come. We appreciate all your support and encouragement. TESS of North Carolina is eternally grateful of the opportunity to serve.

# Developmentally Significant

I have another observation. I think some adults are too absorbed in their daily challenges and obligations to understand the need to pay significant attention to old matters they have moved off their radar, such as those unresolved developmental issues from childhood. The thinking is that if adults have made it this far without treatment, whatever they were dealing with in childhood no longer matters. Besides, if they have children, children today have so many more resources and outlets that adults have been lured into believing that getting themselves together is less of a necessity for their children's health than it was in the past.

Adults can now lose themselves in things they can do outside themselves and make it more purposeful than anything within themselves. Adults become preoccupied in personal groups, clubs, and social Internet sites where they may unconsciously ascribe to an identity and value separate from what they need to do for or with their children. This may give them a status that acknowledges, separates, and insulates them, in a friendly way, from the things and people that once stressed them. Sometimes the people they choose not to be bothered with or stressed with are their children, because adult-child interactions conjure up old childhood issues they want to forget. As adults settle into a new mode, attention to their old developmental issues continues to fade. The appearance of their significance becomes less, yet the reality of their importance never fades and probably increases with the passing of time because now they are at a stage where they can pass on unresolved issues to the innocent.

Passing on unresolved issues is not synonymous with solving old issues. It just means issues are being extended into another generation. We forget that developmental stages in life occur throughout our entire life and do not end with adolescence or even middle age. Again, becoming all consumed in groups, projects, or even substances may insulate but will not annihilate. Time spent running away only amounts to submerging and hiding issues. Some adults are willing to mask their problems in their children. It allows adults to continue doing whatever they are doing with little or no sense of remorse and responsibility. If adults become highly meaningful and respectful in whatever endeavor they thrust themselves in and those around them reinforce that significance, then it is highly likely they may believe they have moved beyond a need to ever address what was once an issue in their lives. Those working with them on the endeavor would never suspect anything lurking beneath the surface. If the adults are perceived as too important to have any serious problems, yet issues persist, the children will pay for the misgivings of the adults.

This process can be repeated over and over and become generational. The rapid changes and offerings in society push us to live and live abundantly, so overindulgence becomes routine and normal. Somehow resulting troubles always ensue from inattention to matters where the can has been repeatedly kicked down the road. The access to more programs unfortunately sometimes mean more time for children to interact with professionals while adults continue their social hobnobbing. Are the children "wilding out" because adults have boxed them in and they have no other way out?

Society is as society is, but adults—who make up society to varying degrees—are shuffling responsibility to innate objects and projects that assure them a front-row seat with blinders and more of the issues they were seeking to escape.

# Developmentally Significant: The Next Generation

Unbeknown to us, certain environmental conditions and situations along with national and cultural factors will serve as a backdrop for nourishment or impediments to a healthy development. Individuals, families, communities, and institutions will provide these impediments or nourishments along a continuum. However, before one gets to such institutions as schools or religious establishments, the immediate and extended family will provide significant age-appropriate skills and mental framing or inadequate age-appropriate skills along with proper or improper mental framing. Neither will offer a guarantee of success or failure, but as one moves out into the greater community and partakes of nourishments or impediments from institutions such as schools, it will be that earliest positive encapsulation that offers the highest percentage for success.

If a child reaches adulthood and is an offspring of an adult with unresolved childhood issues, and that child is in the same or similar community that contributed to that adult's challenges, then that child has a better-than-average chance of repeating the same or similar cycle. That adult teacher/parent who did not address his or her issues is ill equipped with the knowledge or experience to explain how he or she overcame them. Unfortunately, moving to a different era is not enough to erase unresolved challenges.

Let's review some fixtures—the things that are not likely to change in a person's life, at least not immediately: the family, community, and school. These three factors are not chosen by the child, yet they affect behavior significantly. Separately, any one of them can be a game changer, but together, they are not insurmountable factors in development because they all represent external factors. Initially, we must work on moving a mindset from recognition of barriers as constraints and complaints to a mindset that recognizes barriers as constants in life masking as unfriendly occupants designed to heighten and crystallize desire and determination. In working with youths with deep-seated, unresolved generational issues, it is unlikely we will be able to affect the external factors with any degree of effectiveness, at least not immediately, so our best bet is to identify, access, and mobilize their internal strengths. The earlier we do this the better.

We have to teach how to operate in the mud without becoming muddy, how to dance in the rain without getting wet. It is a mindset that makes obstacles, expectancies, and external factors become ex-factors. The family and community will probably continue to serve as a conduit for inappropriate development. We must search for opportunities to pair or expose individuals with people and situations throughout the community, state, nation, and world with life experiences that allow them to reframe their barriers as opportunities. Sometimes when we look closer at people, we notice that the constants that seem to separate achievers from non-achievers are not unusually different, nor is there an absence of barriers, because barriers are constants for everyone to one degree or another. The achievers made those external factors partners and allies, but it started from within. Moving an individual who has demonstrated characteristics of laziness or uncleanness into a new job or new mansion will only serve to imbue those characteristics on that new job and new house if changes are not made from within.

Time is the only factor missing from revealing those results. The passing of time will surely disclose the outcome of what is within. The house and job will receive the same fate as previous houses and jobs if that change is not made within. All changes that are significant changes must be made from within first before they can reveal a positive outward result. Adults with children have biological scapegoats and find them very useful in camouflaging their issues. My child is lazy, dirty, or can't keep a job. It is the adult requirements of life and a greater level of maturity that accounts for the small difference in the adult and the child. All the wisdom and social etiquette acquired en route to adult-hood cannot cover up the developmental issues still present in the be-haviors, actions, and characteristics of the adults. The recognition and acknowledgment of that by adults is the first step in the confirmation that the change is going to come.

# Happiness Ever After

I am often confronted with a variety of individuals who are upset about not being able to find happiness, but in conversation after conversation, I discover they expect to find happiness by using formulas that eliminate themselves as determinants and relevant factors. I am often accused of acting like solutions are so simple that it appears I am making light of their situation. Happiness is not a destination, but a process. My intent is not to insult, but I would like to ask that we study how we expect to become a part of a process for ourselves by zeroing ourselves out of the process. Happiness for individuals is routinely expected to be determined by something or someone out there. It means something from out there is necessary for happiness to occur. This missing piece must be brought into the individual. Yet, somehow, the individual is just a conduit with no active role.

We attempt to extrapolate a desired function (happiness) from an external determinant, and then superimpose that determinant onto the individual as a condition while the individual acts as a receiver. The continuation of that happiness is dependent on the permanence of that external determinant. The individual had no role in bringing it about and has no role in maintaining it, but should somehow expect happiness forever. This is counter to pre-elementary logic. In the words of George W. Bush, who said he had a bead on it, Mr. President, I need your help to get a bead on this one. When an individual's happiness is independent of the individual and dependent on someone else, some other place, something else, or some condition out there, happiness will forever elude that individual or, at a minimum, it will be short-lived and disingenuous.

# Perfect Call

No one is perfect. Most people are willing to agree with that statement and admit they are not perfect. So at least from this point, we have set a tone of agreement. Yet contradictions ensue almost immediately because very few of those same people are willing to admit to circumstances and situations when they were not perfect. Admitting the first statement should automatically cement an agreement on the existence of shortfalls. It would also create a framework for less defensiveness. From that admission we can begin to identify some areas of imperfections that we all have and see how we can work together to improve them.

In this vein, we can begin examining how decisions, regardless of why we think we made them, lie with each and every one of us and we can study how they have yielded rewards or consequences in the exact manner and proportion of how they were made. Now for those who profess to not be perfect but are still unable to admit any specific imperfections or wrongdoings, we must call you perfect. This is about the log in your own eye.

# Tiger Blood

Now, suppose you find yourself on a fast-moving tiger and you have been holding on for quite some time, but the current dangers and the pending disaster (upcoming cliff) alert you that you must dismount soon. You look to your left and see a row of cactus; to your right is a small canal with what appears to be water at the bottom, but you cannot tell how much. The cliff is fast approaching so you must make a decision. What are your choices? How many choices do you have? Most people say they have two choices, the right or the left. Some have told me that they have no choice, that all the choices belong to the tiger.

In fact, the choices are many. Some of the choices may be limited by your current skills, however. In considering the right side, can you swim if the depth of the canal makes it necessary? Is the slope of the canal such that you can climb back out if you are injured? Do you know anything about tuck-and-roll that would be beneficial in facilitating your descent on the left or right? Have you appropriately surveyed both sides to determine the best place to dismount? Is there anything you can do to slow the tiger or even stop the tiger before he reaches the cliff? Can you ride the tiger down to the bottom of the cliff, and what would be your chances of survival? And lastly, are you prayed up and paid up?

There are probably more choices than the ones I mentioned, but the purpose of this exercise is to emphasize the many choices that are available to us in life.

When one is in a crisis or survival mode, how one got on the tiger must be suspended until the storm of the ride subsides. Provided you survive this ride, it is most important that we discuss how you got on the tiger, because the survival rate on each succeeding tiger ride goes down exponentially.

# What's in a Dropout?

A child enters a race for academic procurement. When the child enters, the child is much too young to understand the gravity and significance of what that first day of school means. The child's understanding at this particular junction is not a prerequisite for a successful start. However, it would be very helpful if the child's parent(s) or other significant others in the child's life understood the gravity and significance of the day. The child may already be behind. The child may not know that but the adults should. If a child is behind in a race, there seems to be only two ways to catch up: run faster (work harder) than the children ahead of him, or facilitate a slowdown or stoppage of the children ahead of him. The latter may not be as feasible as the former. If one or both of these are left undone, the child who started behind stays behind.

If the adults who brought the child to school believe the race started on the first day of school, it still holds true that it is the child who is behind but, because this is an adult-initiated issue, it will require the adults' assistance to get the child up to speed and on pace to compete with those ahead of the child. But, hold up, if these are the same adults responsible for the child being behind in the first place, are these adults capable and can we really count on them to do more (which is what is required now) of what they didn't do initially in order for this child to at least be on grade level? The adults, well meaning, did not do what should have been done because they just were not up to the task and, frankly, they still aren't, but they got the child to school and now they may wash their hands of the situation and hold the school accountable from this point forward. So the child, from day one, was on pace to drop out and was more prepared for dropping out of the race than competing and completing the race. So it is the child who drops out in middle school or high school, but it is the adults who prepared the child for dropout, and it is the school that continued the child on the slow and late pace that he entered.

The school used a flawed baseline (a baseline that was perhaps created by parental ineptness) and slowed the child even more with accommodations and modifications, which only made the child mimic the pace of the children ahead of him. Slowing the child down is incompatible with the things I mentioned earlier that are necessary for the child to catch up. The child started full of energy, ready to compete but unaware of his deficits. Somewhere in the race, the child realized things were not going very well for him. The child began falling farther and farther behind. The child noticed he was getting lost and unnoticed. He began to act up to make himself more relevant, but instead, this inflamed those championing his effort to side with those preparing to throw in the towel.

As people began to give up on him, he realized less time, energy, and resources were being spent on him and his kind. He detected that people at home, school, and the community were now taking bets against him finishing the race and, although he had not admitted it to anyone, he was beginning to have his own doubts. Some of his friends were passing the finish line and moving on. Younger siblings were easing up and beginning to catch him, yet the finish line was not in sight. To save face, the child who started the race full of promise, but behind, declines, and drops out. The child is counted among that increasing number of dropouts and nowhere is it listed as an adult or parental-assisted dropout. From the start, the odds were against this child, but beating the odds must become the mantra of every such child. Completing high school is a part of a process that is integrated in a lifetime process, so dropping out of school ends only the academic race with the children with which the student started, so it seems, but not monitoring and keeping pace with the peers around the globe may be even more catastrophic.

Slowing down or stopping by the child keeps the child getting farther and farther behind. Now that the child is an adult, what is the adult going to do to ensure that this adult does not bring another child to the first day of school behind and unable to compete and complete the race for academic procurement? Of course, the race did not start at the child's first day of school or the child's adult caregiver's first day of school. The race also did not stop when the child dropped out of school. Once in the race, obsessing about when and where it started is pointless. The deceleration or stoppage as an adult or child may demonstrate indifference to the race, but it is immaterial to the existence of the race. The race is never static. Whether an adult or child, the choices are the same: run faster, facilitate a slowdown or stoppage of those ahead, or get farther and farther behind. The race is endless and not optional; competing is endless and not optional.

# Poverty: Blessing or Curse?

Born in poverty, surrounded by ill-equipped parents, schools, and communities, and cut off from cultural and environmental advantages—a poster child for at-risk behavior . . . Do we say, game, set, match—it is over? Situations and conditions of birth and upbringing are not the choices of the individuals who encounter them but they will impact their development. The challenge I see is one of paradigms and habits created by that environment and reinforced by the very environment that created them. How about a paradigm shift in thinking and a character check that puts all those aforementioned disadvantages at risk of being run over by the poster child?

# How Great Thou Are

My approach seems simple because, again, I want to start with something I think many can agree on. "Greater is He that is in me than he that is in the world." Now, if you believe that, then all the factors external to you combined are lesser than what is within you. It renders the magnitudes of all tasks and obstacles powerless. I have learned that a person's belief and understanding of oneself determines the limits of the achievement, yet it is often unrelated to the person's true greatness. Yet fear and the belief in the strength of obstacles often limit that level of greatness. One must meet a person where he is in his thinking, and it is difficult to move a person beyond where he is mostly because of fear that appears to be a by-product of rearing and environment. All have various levels of this deficit, and sometimes a reasonable level can be useful. Yet, in some cases, without the proper counsel and motivation, one may choose not to expand on that greatness, which, again, has nothing to do with the greatness itself.

If someone told me I had the capacity to fly a jumbo jet and they can assure me it would not be a deficit of mine in three months, I may find that a challenge I wish to decline. I may quote various reasons but the underlining reason would probably be fear. Then, I am told within one year, my current land of inhabitance will no longer support life and I have been selected to use a jumbo jet to get others and myself to a new land. All of a sudden, I have not changed in height, weight, or any other measurement, but the change is measurable in the sense that I am now willing to tap into that which was always in me that is greater in me than anything or any obstacle that is exterior to me.

When we observe the fear and trepidation in others, we must connect and pair the size and scope of the task to their level of functioning at the time, so when a task of an extreme level of difficulty confronts an average-skilled individual, that individual generally fares about the same as any other individual facing a skill deficit. A child's fear of taking that first step, relatively speaking, is on the same scale as an adult's fear of jumping out of a plane for the first time or a bird taking his first flight from the nest. All fear is the same in that sense. If one succumbs, it renders its occupant immobile. Our rise in life means we have overcome fear often. Many times throughout life, we have chosen that greatness within to confront and conquer various exterior obstacles without realizing it. No matter the size of the obstacles or the fear associated with it, it all comes back to how in sync we are with "Greater is He that is in me than he that is in the world." The true understanding and application of that greatness within must employ you to move forward with the knowledge that you were born undefeatable.

# Man Up

Man's highly developed mind is what truly separates mankind from the other species and accounts to a great degree for our survival and progress far beyond that of other species. Even in simple things this is apparent.

Imagine that a twelve-year-old child and a full-grown dog are each standing at the edge of a road. Across the road is a burger and fries for the child and kibbles and bits for the dog. An average developed and hungry child will assess the traffic in both directions before crossing the street. In that same situation, an average dog will probably throw caution to the wind and dash full speed across the street. If the stars are properly aligned in his favor, he gets to eat; if they are not, the buzzards get to eat, and so this would end the progress of his generation. Now our ability to reason and process must be utilized to obtain the benefit. When we fail to use this capacity, we relegate ourselves to the same alleged status of other species, and are subject to the same or similar consequences.

To expand on this a little further, I believe this is what constitutes man's seemingly great separation from the other species. Genetically and biologically, we have more of the same essential features necessary for life. For the most part, we all need water, nourishment, shelter, and oxygen. We all bleed a similar fluid when cut or bruised and continuous bleeding without intervention to stop it will lead to the death of that species. Because of man's highly developed mind combined with the passing of time, we have been able to thrust ourselves so far ahead and above the other species that it appears we belong in a different category altogether.

We are the only species I am aware of that can take the accomplishment of one generation and advance that accomplishment and repeat that process indefinitely, as with the Wright brothers' airplane and the caveman's first weapon. This advancement may be good or bad, comparatively speaking, for example, the caveman's spear and today's weapons of mass destruction. I believe that no amount of human progress can or will elevate man beyond the base of who he is or what he is naturally relative to the other species. Essentially, as defined by nature, the separation of man and other species has not widened, only the appearance has, and time cannot discount that fact; it only confirms it. Our advances in technology, absence a few years added to our lifespan, have done very little relative to our core nature qualities.

Man's accomplishments have created an inflated sense of importance over the centuries to the point that man has subtracted and added days to the months and even inserted months into the year. No other species would ever attempt such an excursion into nature, and even if it were possible by other species, man would forbid it and certainly would not comply with any changes. In recent years, man has instituted and manipulated daylight savings time to his benefit. If the change that benefits man adversely affects the habitation of any other species, man's assessment of how it affects his species will probably determine the future action of man and not the ecosystem's realities. Such action by man, though seemingly significant, has only affected clock and calendar time. The accumulations of centuries of man's feats and actions have done absolutely nothing to the natural course of time. In fact, man is not the beginning and end of anything. He is only a part of something. Man's relationship and sense of value relative to that something is unchanged by his actions and achievements, no matter how they are viewed by history, which, itself, is an illusion of grandeur.

# A Structured Settlement

One thing that seems clear and obvious to me is that children of all eras and in all parts of the world tend to benefit from structure. There was a time when life itself, at least in my upbringing, presented a level of structure that afforded parents some assistance and relief in that area.

A case in point: My parents did not have to structure my time or set boundaries for my siblings and me when it came to the use of the telephone; we did not have a telephone. This meant my parents did not have to monitor this device for negativity. Consequently, there were no problems stemming from three-way or four-way phone usage because we had no-way.

Another case in point: Early in my childhood, we did not have a television. There was, thus, no need to monitor that invention for adverse effects. When we did get a television, we were able to get only one small black and white. We had three network channels at the time: ABC, NBC, and CBS. Many times we were only able to get reception on one channel and sometimes two—when the rabbit ears would work and we had enough aluminum foil to spare. During that time, television signed off at 11:30 p.m. and signed on at 7:00 a.m. The sign-off and sign-on times were different by regions throughout the country. However, it did provide a built-in structure that is not available to parents today.

Radio stations also signed on and signed off during that period. It is reported the word "Internet" wasn't used until 1982 so, of course, my parents had it made again on this one as far as monitoring it for unhealthy residues. Limited accessibility does mean a certain level of structure and boundaries per limitations. This is applicable and meaningful for all forms of communications. However, it does not mean that parents were exempt from all concerns associated with providing structure and boundaries; it just meant they had fewer things to account for when it came to structuring a household, and that they received collaterals from that era.

I don't know of a time period when it was advisable for parents not to structure the environment of their children, yet unstructured environments appear to be so rampant that they have become the norm. Unfortunately, some parents have joined their children in a mindless foray of activities that is counter to the healthy development of their children. Over the last fifty years, there has been a tremendous increase in media and communications equipment, and it is imperative that parents and adults respond to that increase with courage, vigilance, and creativity. For parent and adults who have thrown up their hands claiming there are too many meaningful pieces to manage, I am going to offer a structured settlement. All structures and boundaries must begin in the home. There is some managing that can be effective even in a period where there appears to be unlimited access to the world from almost any where in the world. The teaching and cognitive element of that structure must begin early, and it must be consistent. It is more important than the physical aspects.

Almost all equipment and items utilized in accessing the world—cell phones, televisions, computers, iPads, etc.—are purchased by adults or parents, which means they are the OO (Original Owner). The OO can structure when these items are acquired, and when, how, and where they will be utilized. That determination should not be made due to the amount of pleas or tears presented by the child or because of how exhausted the OO is from the previous or current day's work. Maintaining ownership of your products also means you are always the OG (Original Guardian) of all things that matter in and outside of your home. When parents allow children to have free range to any and all devices purchased by the parents, it translates into a childhood ownership and management program that almost always amounts to children run amok with serious structural and boundary deficits. Parents are the drivers and the children are the passengers. The reason the children are driving the parents crazy is because the children have worked their way into the driver's seat, and parents are either trying to negotiate from the passenger side or they have been put out of the car altogether. Expecting a return of a time period when built-in structure may have sufficed is expecting a bygone era to return. It is time to initiate a structured settlement.

# Is It Right or Is It Fair?

In the matter of right and wrong, the prevailing argument seems to be that it depends on whose perspective from which we are viewing it. That ensures that it remains convoluted. Then there is Nike's advertisement that image is everything. It makes right and fair nothing more than flair. Many love to pair right with fair as equals, and I often hear kids arguing back and forth about the rightness and fairness of a particular thing as if they are one and the same. The fairness thing, in my mind, is not very difficult to access if we are referring to people getting the same thing.

At birth, this matter is doled out unfairly by those standards, so who are we to expect that we, a part of the nature that is doled out, should right a matter already distributed by nature? Some are born blind, deaf, minus limbs, or with some mental deficit. Is this fair? It is fair, relative to the fact that naturally each and every one is born with a degree of advantages and deficits relative to chance, and that the chance of one being born either way is not leveraged by the action of the one being born or the person giving birth. Fair has more to do with need than right or wrong. If I need a hearing aid and you don't, imposing that requirement on you for the sake of fairness seems rather ridiculous to me.

Right and wrong is a little more complicated, but I think when we access right and wrong on a singular basis, important factors are mangled and smeared with prejudices and biases, and when personally measured, these important factors are passed off as unimportant and irrelevant to the outcome because it feels right. It was right for me to slap him for being in my space, and when we elicit a review, it is generally from others of like minds or from a like-minded group so, of course, there is a reinforcement of the correctness of the position, and if egos are ruffled, then clarity is permanently blurred. As such situations are multiplied on a case-by-case basis, the passing of time may even normalize it to the point it no longer needs a review. Watch out, it could become a custom.

I propose we multiply that single case of slapping someone for being in one's space and assess its contribution to the betterment or detriment of mankind or all-kind. I would use all-kind if the action or behavior were applicable to all species. The value and significance of our connections to one another gets lost too quickly when we keep things on a singular or personal basis. If this is not done, we get in more arguments about what is too close and so forth, and the rightness and wrongness of the action becomes too subjective to ever get an answer. Aligning ourselves in a single group and acting as one and viewing the actions of that group from a single perspective or single mind-set tend to blur the issue of right and wrong.

The alignment of other nationalities under their single national interest or cause represented several single groups' mindset that accounted for the righteous killing of nearly sixty million people in WWII. Somehow, only man—the so-called highest order of life, with his advanced and complex minds and systems—is routinely guilty of killing and maiming millions over and over again under the banner of nation building or ethnic cleansing. Man compartmentalizes right and wrong into separate groups and raises the level of consideration of one group's interest above the consideration of another group. A part becomes more important than the whole because the betterment or detriment of mankind is now subject to consideration only after the interest of the superior group is satisfied. Right and wrong becomes subject to challenges from other groups jostling for a more superior status. Right and wrong revert back to my opening statement about whose perspective we are using. This makes it too speculative to measure with any degree of accuracy.

A better determination of right and wrong is derived by taking an act or behavior out of its singular form, multiplying it by thousands or millions, and then honestly assessing it for its contribution to the betterment or detriment of mankind or all-kind. This formula is useful for the action and behavior of other species, although it appears the lesser orders of life would derive more benefit if man would observe the formula.

# The War Against Drugs/Medication

I am not a doctor, and I have never played one on TV or anywhere else, for that matter. Please consult with your physician before beginning, discontinuing, adding, or making any changes with prescription drugs; I do. I currently take medication for hypertension, so I am certainly not opposed to taking medicine. I realize that medication has provided many with relief from certain ailments as well as contributed to a higher quality of life. That may have not been possible had it not been for their physician and the right medication. Herein lies the dilemma. Can the very things that are good be bad?

Let's take alcohol as a drug, which has long been thought to be useful for pain and other matters, especially in the Old West. Even today, a person with some social inhibitions or shyness may experience some benefit from that anxiety during social gatherings. A small shot (dosage) of the right alcohol (drug) may very well lighten things up for him. So the alcohol acts as a social lubricant and does what it is given (prescribed) to do. It works and works fairly quickly. In a lot of cases when medication is given (prescribed) and is taken in the manner it should be taken, there are transformations that are measureable, and no other discipline can argue against that truth.

Notice, I make no distinction between nontraditional, legal, or illegal drugs. Drugs, labeled medicine, over-the-counter, prescribed, or street, are all drugs and must be viewed as such. Ritalin, which is commonly prescribed for ADHD, is "speed," a Food and Drug Administration (FDA) Schedule II drug. It is pharmacologically classified with amphetamines, cocaine, and methylphenidate, and it has some of the same addictive properties. But back to the person with the alcohol; he has found his cure for his anxiety—or has he? What he was first given (prescribed) is no longer having the desired effect, so he must take an increased shot (dosage) or change his brand (prescription) to get the effect he once got. His body has made an adjustment to the alcohol (drug/medication); therefore, he must make an adjustment. It now looks like he has relapsed because his anxiety has made a comeback.

Can we win or outrun this condition (anxiety) with a steady increase in the various brands and dosages available to us? It is well documented that people have been using alcohol and other drugs to self-medicate for years. We also have evidence on how well that has been working. If the very amount or dosage that was given to the first gentleman that made him the life of the party is increased too rapidly or in too large of a quantity, that same drug that produced such a wonderful result for him may also cause a blackout or even death.

Unfortunately, our unconscious reliance on medication has created a climate where individuals and their families look to medication first, second, and last for a quick fix for an array of issues. I find it a little perplexing that environmentally induced conditions with a medical rule-out require a medical solution. It is akin to medicating a person for loss of weight that stems from excessive worry, anxiety, and feelings of hopelessness due to long-term unemployment and years of living in an environment of poverty and violence. A person in this situation may gladly submit to medication just to pause the whirlwind and avalanche of mayhem. And who am I or anyone else to say it is not a good call, especially if suicide was her next option?

Yet, sometimes, when medication brings a pause in the negative action, it signals that it is business as usual, similar to a man who goes back to eating salt and pork once his blood pressure is brought under control by medication. The core conditions (joblessness, poverty, violent environment) or the behaviors (poor planning, bad decision making, lack of discipline) that contributed to these symptoms are not addressed by medication. I talked to a lady once who advised me that at one time she was on as many as twenty-five different medications and that she was in worse shape than she was at the time I was talking with her. I couldn't help but think, how did she keep up with the times and dosages of twenty-five medicines when I saw her having trouble keeping up with three; yet, for medication to work best it must be taken as prescribed.

Another concern of mine is the seemingly alarming rate and age with which we are medicating children. Why are we generally opposed to our children drinking coffee (caffeine) and ensuring that we have laws that disallow our children to smoke cigarettes (nicotine) before age eighteen even if our children are stressed, yet we are okay with our children taking medication (drugs) at almost any age? As I mentioned earlier, I think environment has a lot to do with behavior, and children are certainly not excluded from the effects of their environment. The developmental influence appears to be more refined during childhood. There may be a similar range in the development for most children, but some seem to follow a different beat and path along many different pathways (for example, emotional, cognitive, language), and that difference, which may be normal for that particular child, may get medicated because it does not fit with society's norms.

People do not learn anything new from taking medication. Well, perhaps they learn they feel better, or it confirms they needed medication, or that maybe there was something wrong with them and they believed medication fixed it. For a child to learn that, and learn that the parent assisted with acquiring that knowledge, could amount to a developmental stranglehold. Issues that are certified early in the life of a child tend to mount, and by the late teen years, there are too many to control with one medication. Remember, the body adjusts to medications; I am certainly not on the same medication I started on a few years ago. Medications require constant reviewing and monitoring for the proper adjustment to be made. Practically all medications have side effects, even if they are minimal. If the side effects are more troublesome than the fixes, then something must be done to address the side effects. If medications are changed, upgraded, or added even if it is because a medication lost its patent protection or there was a change on the preferred medication list, a child who started early may enter adulthood taking a lot of medication. As medications are added to counter the various side effects, it means the number of prescriptions increase, and the original problem may no longer be the major problem. The mental health industry appears to allow the unlimited use of medication, without prior approval, even if a person has been taking medication unsuccessfully for years. Yet, behavioral interventions that must have prior approvals, are limited to a few months and must have a strict measurement or research standard for success.

According to a September 2008 Kaiser Family Foundation report, pharmaceutical manufacturing was the most profitable industry from 1995–2002. In many of the communities I travel, there appears to be a noticeable change or increase in the amount of pharmacy stores that occupy corner lots. I think it is important that we educate ourselves and our families in the proper review and use of medication for the prevention and maintenance of illnesses and diseases. Let's not confuse "Hooked on Medication" with "Hooked on Phonics." An industry that spends over ten billion dollars a year in advertising alone is a heavily invested industry, and for you not to invest some time in knowing what that may mean for you may be a part of that poor planning and bad decision making that makes and keeps you a candidate for their product.

I think as a society we gravitate to drugs because people and institutions are in a fast-paced and competitive mode or climate and are clamoring for instant results. In the classroom or boardroom, the cry is the same. Give me results, and anything or anybody that is a hindrance to those results must be handled in the most expedient fashion so we can get back to the business of teaching or running this company, or we are going to lose this global race for supremacy. The trade-off for expediency is often quality. There have always been causalities in wars— and some people are going to get hurt, mauled, maimed, or even killed along the way—but make no mistake about it, we will win this war.

One other factor that plays into my thinking is that as a country we have gotten too fat, comfortable, and lazy to work to combat those conditions that ail us, and we are quick to hand over our problems and the problems of our children to anyone or anything that alleges a fix; if they have M.D. at the end of their name, then that just means

My Dawg. I need something that works and works quickly because I am a part of the now generation. A man comes into an office complex, and he is out of control, behaviorally. Nobody seems to be able to calm him down. The doctor comes in and administers a Haldol shot and the irate man calms right on down. The problem has been averted, the doctor receives the award for best practice, and all other professionals are saying they needed more time; a commodity that is sadly no longer recommended. A well-placed baseball bat to the back of the head would garnish similar results, with the same side effects of headache and dizziness, but maybe a lump would be an additional side effect. Also, with the baseball bat, there are no lingering addiction concerns. It is similar to the matter of lethal injection or hanging; they both work. Which one will leave you with the least collateral damage?

In the mental health field, it is all about controlling or managing behavior. We use medication simply because it works, and it appears to be the quickest and best fit for allowing us to compete and complete our other important tasks, whether they are in the classroom, home, office, community, or any other place where people gather. Please do not forget the addiction factor. Many of those who take medications for various issues are some of the same folks who drink, smoke, take other drugs, and otherwise make poor decisions and choices in other areas of their lives, and this may expedite the addiction or poisonous process. Medicating the very young appears to have increased in recent years. Are our eyes open to who is being medicated and the long-term implications of our choices? Do we know what's going to be in the can that we are kicking down the road when we open it down the road?

Medication is most effective when it is used to prevent conditions. Conditions are most effective when lifestyle and decision-making can prevent medication. By not taking the time to educate ourselves about environmental and developmental issues and not investing the time to teach and promote the use of coping skills and strategies for long-term conditions and circumstances, we are settling for short-term approaches and using the same poor planning and bad decision making that prompts a need for medication in the first place . . . but then, maybe that is the plan.

# Youthful Indiscretion

To be young is to be captivated by an era and sense of exuberance absent a level of maturity often unknown and undetected by the youth. The lack of years utilized in gathering experiences renders youth incapable of accessing density and layers of relevant information as it relates to situations and their relationship to future outcomes. This is a time when we believe the world is our oyster; we know everything and can do anything.

To be honest, although the odds are against us, with an adequate amount of knowledge and counsel and a dream, we may have the energy and drive to obtain the riches of the world. What profit will a person have if he gains the whole world and forfeits his life? "Lean not unto thine own understanding" comes to mind here. But for the youth, their understanding is not only the most important understanding it is the only understanding. This understanding is reinforced by a culture of economics and systemic structures that cater to the interest of youthfulness with the same complacency and disregard as that of the youth. With systems and economics as they are and with the benefits that are derived from the youth as they are, I don't think a review or reversal of current matters are in the works any time soon.

When I was eighteen I thought as I was eighteen, and to have asked me to think as if I was forty-eight would have been most difficult and akin to asking me to think as a female. My day-to-day grind at forty-eight and my day-to-day grind as a female were both zero, and as much as I may have tried to put myself in the shoes of each, they would have been too tainted by my day-to-day experiences at eighteen to have had any real worth.

So, how do we get the youth to operate with more discretion and with better judgment when they are inherently disadvantaged by their youth, sometimes to the detriment of us all? When I was in my early twenties, I really thought I knew a lot, but I used to pass my parents' house on my way to my girlfriend's house, always promising myself that I would stop in on my way back or that I would stop the next time. The next time would rarely come, or it would be too late to stop on my return trip. At the time my mother had already been diagnosed with breast cancer and was receiving treatment. I was either in denial about how little time we had left together, or I was just too dumb to know how much I didn't know.

If we only knew how much we don't know; that is the question that is begged of all youth. They get married in their late teens or early twenties against the counsel of everyone including the family pet, and then they wonder what happened a year later. How the youth think of and use sex is akin to how drinking partners use each other. Take out the alcohol and they don't have anything in common; they have no use for each other. Take the sex out of a relationship and they may not even like each other. This is also why in the later years of life as sex wanes, for some, that is, partners really enjoy each other because their relationship becomes more about each other and less about sex. When the union is not conditioned by sex from either partner, the relationship stands a better change of functioning properly. Youthfulness, many times, renders this more meaningful relationship impossible. Money is also at the top of the list in failed youthful relationships. Many times what they know about money, absent spending it, is just absent.

# Traditional Marriage

Using "traditional" and "marriage" in the same sentence has almost become profane in some circles. To those whom I offend, this chapter should be the least of your offended worries. Marriage is serious business and should always be treated with seriousness. This is an arena only mature adults should step into. It must be based on true love. That love may not be redefined as anything but those matters centered on mutual respect, trust, honesty, and eternal loyalty to each other. It must be first and foremost to all other human relationships. This means no other human relationship is ever held in higher regard, respect, or admiration. Joint communication and a permanent commitment to these principles are required.

Individual freedom is a necessary ingredient if both parties are to grow and flourish. When freedom is responsibly exercised, an atmosphere for personal growth and happiness will exist. Spousal demands that hinder or limit the freedom of mature individuals committed to the same purpose not only limits free and lively contribution to that purpose, it forces a conscious and unconscious battle with the oppressive one. A by-product of this is resentment, which is counterproductive to the longevity of the marriage. Freedom in marriage is a requirement, but it must be openly tied to self-directed responsibility and accountability. The sanctity of the marriage must never be compromised. The use of chemicals and other mind-altering substances that dull memory or interfere with judgment is ill-advised. Nevertheless, it does not relieve one of responsibility or accountability when exercising freedom in marriage.

The specifics of lovemaking (sex, intimate kissing, and intimate caressing) are exclusively reserved for the marriage, and such activities in concert with others must never be included in the exercise of freedom. Tinkering with this union in this manner temporarily relegates the marriage from first to some lesser order of importance, mobilizing a division in mental energy. The continuations of such an affair will likely lead to a diversion of financial funds earmarked for the marriage. Engaging in what is called "running around on each other" while married is like drinking and driving—they don't mix.

The passage of time and scrambled circumstances will further cloud judgment and purpose. Stay focused. Realize that a marriage worth having is worth working hard to maintain. A lifetime commitment can only be fulfilled one day at a time. Sometimes pondering the trisection of allure, bliss, and wondrous challenges "out there" against the specter of a future with questions will prompt premature or ill-advised changes in humans. All future situations amass questions, and uncertainty is a common element endured by all.

Man must be the leader in the marriage and the household, leading by example. He cannot lead from the couch or with a remote control. "Bring home the bacon" must be an action motto. He must be willing to serve those he wishes to lead. He must always keep the marriage's best interests at heart. Personal or individual desires must always bow when in conflict with the interest of the marriage. The husband must embrace and foster an environment that not only allows freedom of expression of ideas, but also encourages them. Disagreements should always be handled with rules and within defined boundaries. Profanity, personal attacks, degrading words, and certainly physical exchanges should never be displayed with the emotion of anger.

Daily emotional and verbal expressions of love are a must. Also, barring separation by location, not a day should pass without a physical expression of love. Previous unpleasant events during the day should never be used as reasons for noncompliance to the rule of a daily expression of love. The assignment of anger or other negative emotions to behavior instead of the person will alleviate the desire for retaliation or other long-term negative responses, such as the "silent treatment." If a husband and wife reach a deadlock after an appropriately lengthy discussion, the husband is saddled with the responsibility of making the decision. He may reason that the wife holds a better position, and his position should bow. This does not relieve either of the responsibility or accountability of that decision. If that decision eventually yields a poor outcome, it is not a matter for future discussion.

As mentioned earlier, the husband and wife must always be number one in importance to each other. They should be each other's best friend. No significant secret should ever be shared with anyone else that can't be shared with each other—to do so, especially on a continuing basis, will undermine the "first in importance" relationship.

No one can take advantage of the spouse but the spouse. Our vows both to and for each other are taken by each spouse against the world. No one else in the world took that vow or oath to honor that "first in importance" relationship; therefore, all others are incapable of taking advantage of or violating a vow they didn't take.

When a man chooses a woman as his wife and a woman chooses a man as her husband, that relationship immediately takes priority over all other human relationships including mother-daughter, father-son, brother-sister, or any other relationship previously thought of as most important. If this is not done and events unfold such that the father and mother pass on and the children grow up and move on, there may not be much left of the husband and wife relationship to salvage.

Children should be made aware of their significance, important role, and proper place in the family scheme. The husband and wife must be on the same page. They must maintain a unified front when others—including their children—make efforts to pit one against the other. Potentially explosive disagreements should be settled outside the earshot of children. Healthy disagreements are encouraged.

The best thing a man can do for his wife is to love her. The best thing a man can do for his children is to love his wife. The best thing a man can do for his community is to love his wife. The best thing a man can do for his country and the world is to love his wife. The multiplication of this process by every man to the point of saturation would rid the world of many of its ills. An improper man/woman relationship is the prelude to an improper or unbalanced home. This prompts an unbalanced community, nation, and world.

When a man and woman refuse or are unable to get it right, it leads to a family of questionable or multiple alignments, such as woman over man, woman without man, child over woman, man without woman, woman and woman, man and man, and man and two women. The list of trials and arrangements are endless. The nontraditional examples have become so plentiful that they have become the norm, which has prompted a culture shift in thinking. "Traditional" has been reduced to discussions and whims. Not much among consenting adults is considered "perverted" anymore, it seems. Many have been blinded by all the mind-boggling confusion, losing sight of the sustaining principles of marriage. These principles have not moved. People and their passions have moved.

In a marriage, two are joined as one. No matter how comfortable or complacent the situation may become over the years, think of thankfulness and appreciation, count your blessings, and maintain a conscious effort to never take each other for granted. Husband and wife cannot take from one another or get over one another without getting over on each other. They must pool their energies and resources. The alternative is disaster.

The husband and wife should take an interest in each other's good-natured interests. This will contribute to growing and developing together. It will eliminate and minimize opportunities for someone unworthy who is looking to share the spotlight with a spouse for reasons unclear, undefined, and inconsistent with the overriding principles of the marriage.

On the subject of physical attraction and its importance to the marriage, it is not all-important, but it is too important to completely overlook. The husband and wife should make a serious and consistent effort to look their best at every age. Exercise, appropriate rest, good nutrition, a healthy lifestyle, and weight control will not only help one look one's best, it will contribute to good health and a better quality of life as the husband and wife age. Barring accidents or unforeseen genetic disorders, the husband's and wife's attention to this area of their lives should greatly outweigh inattentiveness.

Lastly, but most important, a man cannot lead if he is unwilling to be led. A positive relationship with God is much too important to be left out of the household. His religious preference, choice, or sect is not important. However, it must be grounded in wholesomeness and goodness, and not the evil or satanic versions popping up posing as religion. The man must remain plugged in with the Master daily for guidance and strength in all things. A woman cannot and will not tie in wholeheartedly with a man who has gone astray or has no sense of direction. If this is not clear in the man, the destination of the marriage, traditionally, is unknown.

# Wanting

On the subject of out of control wanting, collectives are all gathered in their respective corners yelling and pointing fingers at each other and blaming each other for the mess that the states and national economies are in. The haves say the have-nots want more social programs that are bankrupting the country. The have-nots say the haves are lining up their lobbyists to satisfy a want that is an interest of theirs, such as pharmaceutical or private defense contracts. The have-nots blame the haves for being better connected and using that connection to enrich themselves to the exclusion of everyone else and at the expense of everyone else, yet the have-nots are accused of not taking the time to register to vote and even declining rides to polling stations.

According to the have-nots, the haves are the only ones who can concoct layers of disinformation and subsidiaries to obscure the full extent of their actions. Also, they will always let the politician know their vote has a price. The have-nots further claim that being locked out and underrepresented is a state or condition created by those haves to further the interest of those who have. In this endless bid of wanting, each side blames the other for blocking their interest or advancing only their interest.

# My College Days

When I said college days, maybe you finally settled back, saying to yourself that finally the good stuff will come out. You have been waiting to hear about me frolicking around campus, without a care, crashing all the fraternity and sorority bashes like it was 1999. There were a few parties and events that perhaps got out of hand, but it was certainly no Woodstock; more about that later. But let me tell you how it almost didn't get started.

One cool spring morning in my senior year at Maxton High, I got a call to report to the counselor's office. He basically sat me down and got right to the point. "I think you ought to consider going to college." I was startled. I stared back at him, chuckling while telling him he must be kidding. He told me I was number thirteen in my class and he thought my attitude and disposition would make me perfect for college. No one in my family or community had ever said anything to me or anyone else about me attending college, and here is this guy who didn't know me and had never spoken to me up until this point, telling me I should go to college. I did not even know he knew my name. How would this guy know enough about me to conclude that I was college material, and none of my friends ever mentioned it even in a joking manner?

I left his office that morning and did not dare tell anyone why I was summoned to the counselor's office. And, of course, I did not tell my parents or brothers and sisters. I was certain they would laugh and tease me as if it were an early April fool's joke. So, I almost left high school without making any plans beyond high school except going to work at one of the local factories or to the military as most of my older brothers had.

Right before the end of my senior year, I came up with this elaborate plan that I did not share with anyone. I thought that maybe I could sneak into a technical school and if I didn't make it, then I could just sneak right back out and maybe nobody would notice. It would just be my little secret. Well, I started out in some electronics program, maybe just to get a one-year certificate and go to work. No one in my family or immediate community had gone to college, so I did not have anyone to ask; besides, it kept me in line with keeping it all a secret. When I got to the technical school, to my surprise, the class work was far less difficult than I had imagined, so I contrived another little secret to change my major to an associate degree program, and I thought to myself, who knows—if things work out, I could transfer and sneak right into regular college and no one would ever know.

As I think about that period of my life now, I just think of how me, myself, and I became very good at keeping secrets and how silly the whole thing was.

I graduated with honors, again, yet I still did not believe I belonged in college. So I left Richmond Technical Institute (RTI)—now Richmond Technical College—in Hamlet, North Carolina. About four or five students from Maxton started at RTI at the same time and at the end of two years only two were left, Leonard and me. I was told I could transfer and be a junior, but I was having trouble believing all this, and I thought it was going to be found out sooner or later that I didn't belong in college. To my knowledge, no one knew I had any plans to go to college. You see, I did not tell anyone about my associate degree graduation because I was still unsure about whether or not I belonged. So I sneaked and applied for a transfer to North Carolina Central University in Durham, North Carolina, and to my surprise, I was accepted.

Part of what troubled me about college was the thinking that a mistake was made somewhere by someone that allowed me in college, and that I would be the one to have to pay for that mistake for not letting them know. My father always hit the roof where money was concerned, so I was afraid my action was going to cost the whole family some money troubles. My father made me more nervous by telling me often, "Son, I don't know how you are paying for all this, but I am proud of you." In order to keep him and my mother out of financial trouble, I thought it best that I come clean and tell them about the secrets I had been keeping. My parents were good people and needed to know the truth.

The truth is I did not know anymore what the truth was and did not know how it was going to turn out. I had worked a full-time job in McColl, South Carolina, while carrying a full-time student load, which gave me security and assurances as well as no money worries for me or my parents in junior college. Now I was entering a different chapter. The closer I got to my registration date in regular college, the more I was feeling that I had sneaked as far as I could go. I had braced to hear, "A mistake was made on your high school transcript, we are so sorry; you will have to pay all the money back that you received thus far, and your acceptance here has been withdrawn. Besides, you know you can't afford to go to college."

Finally, the day of reckoning came, and as I stood in line to pay my tuition bill, I was trembling and almost ready to get out of line or, worse yet, tell on myself before my name was called. After the wait, I was told in a friendly voice that I was about a couple hundred dollars short of complete payment even with my grant and the money I had earned from working during the summer. I literally was about to cry, when another lady behind the desk said, "Wait a minute, honey" (that was the best-sounding "honey" I think I ever heard), "I think we still have some work-study jobs available," something I had never heard of at the technical school, "Would you like one of those?"

I was overjoyed, saying, "I will take two, you tell me what I need to do." She gave me a slip of paper and told me to go see Ms. Clark at the student union, and I think I ran over a couple of people trying to get to the student union. You see, she said "I think we have some work-study jobs left," and I could not afford being told they just gave out the last one. Now, I was new on campus, and I am probably the worst person for directions, but I found that student union in record time. When Ms. Clark told me I had the job, I could have French-kissed her for a full thirty minutes because at that very moment I could not think of any other options. Calling my parents would just leave me twenty cents short of what I had before I called. This job gave me just enough hours to maintain my obligation; there was not much money left to enjoy the college life, but that was okay as long as I could stay in school.

For a little over a year things worked very well, then tragedy struck. On November 18, 1978, Greg was driving a vehicle where I was a passenger in the rear seat, along with Sarah. Suddenly the vehicle was struck by what I believe was a city bus. We were returning from a NCCU Eagle–A&T Aggie Classic football game that had been played at Duke University. I was pinned in the car. I lost consciousness. I was told the Jaws of Life was used to extract me from the car. I spent six days in intensive care and twelve or thirteen days at Duke Hospital. I was later told by fellow students who were at the scene that some were saying I was losing a lot of blood fast and wasn't going to make it.

When I came to, my first recollection was being surrounded by people in white, making noises that I could not make out, and I said to myself I must be in Heaven, I am glad to be there, but I just wanted to tell my mother and father how sorry I was about all the trouble I had caused, sneaking into college and messing up everything for everybody. When I came back to my senses and realized that I was not dead, the first visitor I saw was my homeboy, Lynwood. He later said he asked me if he should contact my mother and father and that I said, "What mother and father?" After that response, he thought it best to call someone, quick.

The next day, I remember a visit from my mother, my sisters Julia and Naomi, and my girlfriend Diane. I think maybe my niece Veronica and nephew Sherman might have been old enough to come to the room, but I am not sure. I can recall Diane rubbing my head and me screaming in pain. What I remember most about that experience is that I did not know a person could hurt in so many places until I was in that accident. As I was getting better, I began to wonder if Ms. Clark would keep my job open for me, because after I was finally thinking that I belonged in college, I didn't want to have to drop out of school like this.

As I left the hospital I received all of my belongings, which included the clothes that had been cut off my body. Well, I received almost everything, because when I looked in my wallet for my twenty-dollar bill, it was missing. When I told some of my friends about it, they mentioned something about my head injury, saying, "You haven't had a twenty since you've been here." In college, I knew where every penny was that I had. I guess someone figured I was not going to have a use for it. Anyway, I was grateful to be alive and only asked one person about it when I was being discharged. I wonder if there is a statute of limitation on inquiring and if I could be given accrued interest.

When I returned to school, I learned my slot was still open but I could not work in the condition I was in. I was advised that it could not be held open indefinitely, but the school would try to work with me as best it could. I was told to see if I could get some funding from my family to help me complete the school year. I didn't even bother passing that information on to my parents. I was plenty worried about my future. I told some friends, mainly the ones I worked with. They just listened, but offered no solutions. The next day Denise proposed an idea that could help us both. She advised she had used up all of her allowance, and she could work in my place for half and give me the other half. That would help me stay in school, but leave me with absolutely no pocket change as discretionary funds. I had never had anyone do something so nice for me. I almost fell in love. I never forgot that act of kindness and I don't think she ever knew how much that really meant to me.

I can't leave the college days without sharing some of my exploits, and although they are probably child's play to the exploits of many, I will share them nonetheless. You must remember I was a junior when I stepped on campus, so I was a little more mature than the average freshman. Also, I had a two-year financial exit plan and after consultation with my advisors and reviewing my family support fund, I knew I could not get off course. My room on the college campus was the first time in my life I actually had access to an inside bathroom, although it was not private; in fact, it was open to anyone in the building. It was a step up from what I was used to. I must say coming from a small town and country community, I was set aback a little, no, a lot, when I realized for the first time I was at a school with one male dorm and five or six female dorms, so women were everywhere.

I remember immediately saying to myself, "Self, you better get a grip; either you are going to learn how to function among a lot of females or you are going to go crazy exercising your right as a man (dog) and you are not going to be in school very long." I decided on the first choice, but I did see some friends who lost their way and had to utilize an early exit plan that came without a degree. Even with all of my maturity, nothing could save me from crashing and burning when I arrived at my first swimming class and noticed that I was one of two males in a class of about fifteen. I thought to myself that I did not know Durham had a beach. Where are the sand and waves and who cares? Now, this was probably the easiest class I took my entire time at North Carolina Central, yet it is where I made my lowest grade, a C. How did that happen?

Well, looking back on it, I spent more time helping young ladies across the pool and providing support on their backstroke, or maybe it was their backside, while my freestyle took a nosedive. When I left that class, I could barely make it from side to side of the pool without collapsing and knew little of the written material on breathing techniques, but I remembered Scottie and just about every curve she had . . . and there were many. That experience taught me a lesson on focus, because I was not happy about that C on my transcript.

It took some convincing from one of my buddies about what a great time I would have if I just followed his lead once in awhile and enjoyed college a little more. So, I agreed to attend a fraternity bash with free kegs of beer and plenty of wine coolers. I detested the taste of beer but loved anything sweet, so the wine coolers would do just fine. I decided to just swallow the beer as fast as I could to bypass the taste and then use the wine coolers to chase it. I had no idea what I was doing, and by the end of the night I had no idea who I was or where I was. I don't think I blacked out but some time went missing. I know I drove back to my dorm, and I had to travel past at least three or four stoplights, but I don't remember any of them. According to my roommate,

Chris, I woke him up several times with some crazy nonsense. He said the only thing that kept him from kicking my ass was that I couldn't keep it upright long enough for him to get his foot under it.

The next morning, my head felt like a truck had run over it. When I went to my car later that afternoon, I noticed it straddled about three parking spaces. I asked myself who parked my car like that. You talk about scared straight, this was it for me. Being a criminal justice major, I had studied reconstruction of crime scenes and how manufactured evidence can pose a serious threat to justice. I thought long and hard about the night before and all the "what ifs." What if someone had been killed in the same club I attended that night? What if the murder weapon had been placed in my hands and my fingerprints were the only ones found at the scene and on the weapon? Would I have known not to hold the weapon if someone had asked me? The only thing I could attest to is that I was there. As hard as I tried, I could not remember when I left or my trip back to the dorm. Marvin Gaye's "What's Going On" kept playing over and over in my head, and I didn't have a clue. On that day in 1978, I promised God that I would never waste another one of His days like that.

Another sad and gloomy chapter in life for me was my trysts, or delves into one-night stands. To my surprise, my decision to lay all the cards on the table up front about the nature, extent, and intention of my relationship plans only consummated the arrangements even quicker. I soon found that after a few of these affairs that they were too easy, uninteresting, and unsatisfying. My heart was not in it, and it was just another ominous lesson in succumbing to college-stage pressure or dares. I later found out that most people involved in such arrangements were using aliases, so I didn't really know whom I was dealing with.

Then, something happened that expedited my decision to part ways with this chapter of my life rather abruptly. One afternoon I noticed a lot of commotion on the wing of the hall where most of the football players resided. I asked, "What is going on?" I was told there was a girl in one of the rooms and that she was taking on all comers and she was turning them out two and three at a time. I was told to get in line. I was curious so I eased my way up front and was able to get my head in the door to get a look at this hot tamale. I was flabbergasted; she was one of my previous encounters. I started asking myself, "Is this a regular lifestyle for her? How often has she done this sort of thing? What have I gotten myself into? Did I use protection or what have I contracted?" I could not stop my mind from running back and forth. I did not sleep very well that night and could not wait until the next morning to get checked out. Because I was so shaken, one of my homeboys asked me if I knew the girl, to which I replied, "Of course not." After that close call, I instantaneously removed "one-night stands" from my vocabulary forever.

College days were also known as my "Hoover Days" because it seems all I did was stand in line for food. Once, Teddy Pendergrass brought his Teddy Bears for a concert and all I could do was act out Brandy's "Sittin' Up in My Room" alone. Then he started singing "The Whole Town's Laughing at Me" and I thought to myself, "Now why is he sticking it to me like that?" Just for a second I contemplated jumping out the window, and then I remembered it was only two stories, so why hurt my feelings any more. I thought about how sad a case I was to not even be able to come up with six dollars for a show. It was truly outside my budget.

Before I move on I will say I did find the funds for a couple of shows. The one I remember the most was with Peabo Bryson and Evelyn "Champagne" King. It was rumored that Mr. Bryson did not enjoy his reception with the college audience after appearing after Ms. King, but I found Evelyn divinely suffocating. I thought of several hideous ways to get backstage, but all of them would have me singing the Champagne blues.

Thank God the school offered some educational entertainment in the form of speeches at a price (free) I could afford. I did get to hear Julian Bond, Tony Brown, Louis Farrakhan, Stokely Carmichael, and Wallace Muhammad as well as some others before I left my college days behind. Journalist Tony Brown, I remembered, impressed me the most with his flawless flow and summation of details.

# Opportunity 101

I think we have reached a point in time when we must seriously examine where we are with the significance and value of helping services. In the fifties and sixties, many needed help with access to opportunities. The mindset of the people during that era appeared to be, "I have worked and obtained the same entrance requirement of others, but I am being denied access to the playing field." The mindset of the era today appears to be, "You have plenty, and I am in a bad situation, so you ought to give me this product and link me to this service and that service. I want this gift or this handout. In fact, I am entitled to these things because this is the land of plenty and it is un-American if you don't give it to me." When working with this particular mindset, the more you give, the more they want, and the less they do or expect to do on their behalf. More often than not, you will become the object and blame for their failure when you fail to provide them with a product or service that you provided to someone they knew with similar circumstances. A curtailment in products or services due to a change in your ability to provide will be met with the sharpest criticism because now you are putting your needs ahead of theirs, and that is not fair to them because your needs never mattered to them any way. At some point, they gave their set of problems to you without your knowledge or consent, and the failure to address their problems is your fault. Many have been accused of neglect because they discontinue helping. If you knew you could not help forever or at least until I told you that I no longer needed the help, then why did you start?

When we give without a mutual exchange of similar or equal value, the gift almost always takes something from the individual more valuable than the gift. The cost of the gift is too high. Families have unknowingly sabotaged the intrinsic value of their members by not recognizing the lessons imbedded in denial and delayed gratification.

Struggle is a necessary ingredient for growth. Parents of children today routinely say, "I am not going to ever deny my children the things they want as my parents did me. That was so mean of them." Now that I am better off, I am making good on that promise to myself. My children will never have it as hard as I did. So is making it easier for them making it better for them? Again, we take much more from them than the value of the gift.

We are also discounting the value of productive time spent with our children and exchanging it for more of these pseudo-valued gifts. Even though our children may ask or beg for these things, parental acquiescing amounts to a consented coup whereby the parents routinely relegate their charge of parenting to the whims of the children, and the children, in turn, learn a style of parenting by default from their parents to pass onto their offspring that is not only ineffective but also destructive. The children will never believe they, in fact, initiated that parenting style, and the parents will never believe they dropped the ball. From this style or model, children learn they can have any number of things with little or no effort on their part and that all tough spots will be made easy just by calling on their parents, and "no" is a word reserved for use with their parents. We are reaping what we have sown and, as mentioned in the beginning, it is time we seriously examine all helping services, familial and professional.

# Name the Brand

On some occasions I love to just browse around mainly in female shopping areas to try to broaden my understanding of the opposite sex. I consider that a worthwhile endeavor. Maybe I can become the next Steve Harvey.

I happened to go in a store that sold nothing but purses. I can't remember if it was a holiday, although I know it was not Christmas, but the store was running a sale, and it seemed to be packed. I saw some of the purses had three-and four-digit prices. One lady with three purses draped on her shoulder caught my eye because she was still shopping for more. I decided to approach her to find out if I had missed something. I could not wait to tell all the guys I knew how we have been duped into a shorter life expectancy because of secrets contained in the bowels of female purses. I stood in awe in front of this lady, waiting for the scaffolds of history to be revealed to me, but she simply said, "You got to have these."

Now, I am thinking to myself, "You've got to have blood, water, air, and food, and now I have to add purses to that list?" She did not give me any time for a follow-up question, although if the answer had been anything similar to the first one, I don't know why I would have bothered. She sort of pushed through and waved me off as if I mattered little and was wasting her time by attempting to denigrate a sacred purse-buying ritual. I don't know what I could have been thinking. I moved back and observed some more and realized for the first time that I was truly a minority of a dangerous proportion. The one male who was present when I walked in had come to his senses and left; I was alone with countless females in a buying frenzy. Now, I had just agitated one and got shoved aside so perhaps meddling in the business of four or five more might have brought Five-O, which may have been a good thing for me because I might have needed a rescue if things turned south.

Later that evening, I thought some more about my experience and concluded it is not a good idea to accost customers when they are exercising their freedom to de-stress, but to trample me is a little much. I know this is not just about purses, but about society's value shift that appears to say possession of whatever popular product being discussed will raise the stature of the possessor, and the lack of that product will diminish the stature of the non-possessor commensurate with how society has rated that product. The individual identity is essentially bound up and determined by the assumed value of what is on the feet or draped over the shoulders or around the neck.

Oh, yeah, fellows, let's not forget the tires and rims on the vehicle being driven. Our preoccupation with such trappings has embroiled us in a conundrum that makes the likes of me the enemy and camouflages a real threat to humanity. The simple truth is the love, addiction, and worship of the purse is about our relationship to a greater purse and it is not without consequences.

# Education Anyone?

A community and society are lesser or greater commensurate to the level it is willing to educate its citizenry. When any group is precluded from pursuing its maximum potential in education, all groups in that society are robbed of the potential benefits of the excluded group and both groups lose. Those losses are extended beyond the current generation and community and into eternity.

Education in behavior and character should be taught alongside science and math and given an equal footing in value to the individual and society. A well-mannered child, ignorant of science and math, could contribute to the harmony and betterment of society, while a child well-learned in science and math who is ill-behaved and amasses wealth and status will—by default or purpose—contribute to the corruption and downfall of that society, and the building of more wealth will only serve to cover, validate, and reinforce the false correctness of that position. The dark side of the Wall Street phenomenon is the best example of education minus a moral compass.

# Tragedy Hits Home

On one warm summer afternoon, the family was gathered around a thirteen-inch black-and-white television enjoying an episode of "Sanford and Son" when my aunt Jane burst into the room shouting that Naomi shot Joe. Most of us seemed a little startled but not terribly moved because we had grown accustomed to their active relationship. Thinking that perhaps she shot him in the leg, arm, or toe, and that maybe they would behave better after this, I settled back into my well-worn spot to finish watching the show. Actually, I was a little put off that my aunt interrupted me and made me miss Mr. Sanford call Lamont "you big dummy." I really thought my aunt had the information wrong because she was sketchy with the details, so I thought she meant Naomi shot at him or shot off at the mouth, which was highly possible.

Later, my brother Lenwood and I decided to accompany my aunt Jane to the residence of my brother-in-law and sister in Laurinburg, North Carolina. No one was home but the front door was open, and we pushed our way in and walked gingerly around the house, first in the living room and kitchen and then venturing into the back guest bedroom where I noticed some bloodstains on the carpet near the vent. Still unaware of anything other than a few bloodstains, we decided to go to the hospital to ask around. Because there was no sign of my sister or brother-in-law, I was hoping and expecting to visit them in the hospital to hear all about how their dispute got out of hand and that everything was okay and that he would be dropping all charges as was allowed back then.

When we reached the hospital, my aunt approached the receptionist desk and asked if a Joe Anderson had been admitted to this hospital. The receptionist's exact words have been etched in my memory, "You mean the man with the bullet in his head? Oh, he's dead."

That began an afternoon of absolute horror for me, and I am sure for the rest of the family. My aunt crumpled to the floor, and I tried desperately to hold her up, but my knees were buckling and I was doing everything I could to keep from joining her. I looked across the room and saw my brother Lenwood trying to get a grip on a wall to hold himself up, or maybe he was trying to climb the wall or go through it; all I know is he was struggling and looking very unsteady. Thinking it couldn't get any worse, suddenly it did. As I was consoling my aunt on the floor and helping her into a wheelchair, I raised my head and caught a glimpse of my brother-in-law's mother being wheeled through the back of the emergency room, weeping and crying out, "My baby, oh, God no, not my baby. Why did she have to take my baby, oh, God no."

I suddenly stopped thinking about myself and started crying for her because I knew that within the past nine months she had dealt with the death of her husband and another son. With my aunt needing smelling salts to keep her upright while in the wheelchair, my brother crying and marching back and forth like a soldier with no place to go, and me weeping uncontrollably, this was fast becoming the longest afternoon of my life. It seemed like I was aging fast, and my only hope was that someone would wake me up and tell me it was all just a cruel joke.

After a considerable amount of time, we stumbled our way out of the hospital. I wondered if the evening train that hit us was waiting down the road to finish us off. As we made the fifteen-mile trip back home, I can't remember one word that was spoken by any of us. I don't know about them, but I was still in shock three days later. As we reported the news at home to the family, the terror and shock that gripped me at the hospital was starting all over again and was beginning to permeate every fiber of my being. I was filled with all kinds of emotions I had never felt before, and I did not know what to do with them. I witnessed my father for the first time break down shamelessly and cry like a wet baby. He fell on the bed, saying, "Why, where did I go wrong? I did not raise my kids to do nothing like this. Why, where did I go wrong?"

This also was the first time I noticed the true strength of my mother. She was the one who wept slightly, consoling my father and holding his head in her hands while telling him that everything was going to be all right. This was a time unlike any other I had experienced and unlike anything I have experienced since.

# The Village Concept

My father's house was his mansion. He would remind me often that his rule was the only rule. The unfortunate, or fortunate, part about that is he doled out his rule to anyone and everyone in the community, with the understanding that if they didn't enforce that rule as he would enforce it, then they had to deal with him for dereliction of duty. For me as a younger sibling, it meant I had many bosses in the home and community and that I was never old enough to boss anyone around—except on the few occasions when I tried to boss my two baby sisters, Mary and Linda. They would not listen to me, and often, I had to revert to force to get them to do what I told them, especially Mary, who always thought she was older than me.

Oh yeah, I need to mention this before I move on. I could not get too rough with Linda. In fact, no one could get too rough with Linda. You see, she was the baby and Daddy's little girl. We all knew that we were all in for it if our name was the answer to, "Who's been bothering my baby?" So, Mary was really the only one in the family who I could try to boss around and mostly she wasn't having it.

I also knew that in my father's house one rule stood out above all other rules, and it was put to us bluntly: "You will be better off if you spit in my face than put your hands on your mother." I immediately concluded this probably meant I would end up an amputee or paraplegic if I spit in his face. How could it get any worst, maybe blind? Then he followed it up with, "This world wouldn't be big enough for you to hide in." Now, isn't that the kind of thinking that eventually got Osama bin Laden? Anyway, my oldest sister, Julia, was the one in charge most of the time and the one we looked up to the most. My mother and father delegated much of the discipline to my older siblings. I don't remember my older brothers, Gary Jr. and James Andrews, doing too much disciplining of the younger ones except when they would supervise us in retrieving firewood or doing other outside chores.

Whenever I was with my father at a store, church, or in a field, he would always let people know I was his child and they had carte blanche when it came to corrective action to exact the right behavior out of me. I could not go anywhere in my community where the home rule didn't apply. He often said, "I am not concerned about right; I am just concerned with keeping you right." And the teachers, well, they were saints, and when they spoke, it automatically meant you didn't have anything to say. My father said the teachers were always right and until you get a classroom to be right in, you do what the teacher says. If you want to be right and she says she is right, then all she has to do is put you out. He said it comes back to what I said, she is the only person who can be right in her classroom because if she puts everybody out, she is the last person in her class who is right and all those others who thought they were right are right somewhere else, but not in her classroom. If she tells you to stand on your head, you better be on your head when I get there.

I got the picture and, to this day, it is a part of my frame. For my daddy to have to come to school, he would miss a day's work, which meant he would lose money that he could not afford to lose. He would then have to find and perhaps pay someone to bring him. I knew if he did all that, someone would have to pay him for lost wages and time and since I didn't have any money, the manner in which I would have to pay him was too high.

Now my sister Naomi was as much like my daddy as anyone else in the house, and I hated when she was in charge. Daddy would give her some chores to do, and she would get her switch, march the four youngest ones in front of her, and start making assignments. Sometimes she would put the switch on us before she started handing out assignments. She would beat us like she birthed us, and we were all too afraid to do anything about it. Despite all this she was the sibling I think the four youngest ones enjoyed the most because she was sort of wild and crazy, and youngsters always seem to have the most fun with those who know how to have fun.

As a newlywed, she probably didn't like her younger brothers and sisters always tagging along with her, but we would beg to spend the night with her, and maybe we would get a chance to grill out some hot dogs. I don't remember any other sibling who took up as much time with us. I do recall once when my oldest brother, Gary Jr., the first in our family to get an automobile, took a few of us on a ride in his 1966 283 Chevy Malibu. While on this joyride he appealed to a 442 Oldsmobile for a challenge (I am not sure what he was thinking). That Olds quickly pulled away from us and left us with fumes and memories.

As mentioned earlier, Naomi spent the most time with us and no matter where we went with her, she always made us mind her. Maybe she did that to get some extra abuse time. I never thought of it that way. My mother noticed Naomi was being unfair to us and offered us a way out: "Stand up," she said. But we were afraid.

One day, my brother Lenwood and I concocted a story. At our makeshift closet was a sheet that hung on a string that hid the clothes. One of us was to lure her in front of the sheet and the other was to push her down. As the sheet came down on her, both of us would beat her as long and hard as we could. It worked. After that day, her number of slaves was reduced to two. Naomi was as quick to holler and strike you as my father would if you did not do something fast enough. One day she was straightening her hair with a hot iron and she hollered at Linda to bring her the iron off the stove. In Linda's attempt to bring it to her in a hurry, she either picked it up with some of the hot area exposed and contacting her skin or what she picked it up with was too thin to keep the hotness from burning through to her hand. I am not sure which was the exact reason, but by the time Linda got to Naomi, that iron was too hot for her to continue holding so since Naomi asked for it in a hurry, she got it in a hurry—right on her thigh. I think Linda recognized Naomi had on hot pants that day and she was just trying to complete her attire by adding a hot iron as an accessory. Here is a hot iron to go with your hot pants. Linda also got fired from ever having to bring Naomi a hot iron again.

# A Child's Last Stand

There was a time when I used to routinely get the best of Lenwood when we were playing, and it would turn into a fight. He would run to Daddy for refuge. So, one day my father told him, "If your little brother beats you again and you come crying to me, I am going to give you something to cry about."

A couple of days later I was up to my old tricks. For fun, I jumped my brother Lenwood again, but this time instead of him crumpling and crying, he put a whooping on me. He was throwing baby hooks, upper cups, straight jabs, and right and left crosses in combination. As punctuation to the statement, don't mess with me again, I think he ended it with a body slam and a chokehold. He was getting down like his life depending on it and it won't that serious to me. He was fighting like a madman and I didn't know where he got that from; however, this ended my days of ambushing him, and I never bothered him in that manner after that.

# The Golden Rule

Man has attempted to lend some light and guidance to the wayward ways of mankind for centuries but somehow, centuries later, man is still in need of guidance, maybe more today than yesterday. I have wondered how tons of information on guidance and direction over thousands of years has amounted to insufficient information. How does the most advanced species on the planet keep missing the point on what was supposed to be simple and solved centuries ago?

Take the Golden Rule, for example—not without its critics, and not the one you might think. "Do to the doer to cause that he do thus to you" (Ancient Egyptian/Middle Kingdom 2040–1650 BCE), or "That which you hate to be done to you, do not do to another" (Late Period 664–323 BCE). Every kingdom and period since before Ancient Babylon to the modern era has credited some similar statement, religion, sect, or philosopher's saying as its guide for its people, yet today, these words are still misunderstood. Many will come fresh from their religious gathering where it was the delivered message and cuss another out, but would not want that done unto them, or they will talk about another in a manner they would not want to be talked about.

Why is there such an enormous and consistent disconnection across eras and regions on such a simple matter involving diverse and cerebral men? One of Abraham Lincoln's versions of "Do unto others as you would have them do unto you" is: "When I hear anyone arguing for slavery, I feel a strong impulse to see it tried on him personally." Martin Luther King Jr. put it another way when he said, "Injustice anywhere is a threat to justice everywhere." Buddhism: "Hurt not others in ways that you yourself would find hurtful" (563–483 BC). Hinduism: "Do nothing to thy neighbor which thou would not have them do to thee" (4th century BC). African Traditional Religion (Yoruba): "One going to take a pointed stick to pinch a baby bird should first try it on himself to feel how it hurts." Batha'I Faith: "He should not wish for others that which he doth not wish for himself." Judaism: "What you hate, do not do to anyone." Islam: "No one of you is a believer until he loves for his brother what he loves for himself." In ancient China the Golden Rule existed among all the major philosophical schools: Confucianism, Mohism, and Taoism. Confucius: "Never impose on others what you would not choose for yourself " (551–479 BCE). Hadith: "That which you want for yourself, seek for mankind." Sikhism: "As thou deemst thyself, so deem others." Zoroastrianism: "Whatever is disagreeable to yourself do not do unto others." Scientology: "Try not to do things to others that you would not like them to do to you." Janism: "A man should wander about treating all creatures as he himself would be treated." Native Americans: "Humankind has not woven the web of life. We are but one thread of it. Whatever we do to the web we do to ourselves" (Chief Seattle).

On this matter it seems I could go on for decades explaining our common and spiritual connections in how we should treat each other, but what centuries have been unable to do expecting a few decades of explanations from me to be the smoking gun might be over-optimism on my part.

Philosophers, such as Socrates, Aristotle, Plato, Epictetus, and others have all weighed in on this matter. I guess I will take a whack at it also. Our devotion and commitment to the very things and beliefs that bind us appear to separate and disconnect us at a human level (man's created institutions and entities), which overshadows and confuses the supposedly deeper spiritual level (omnipotence and universality). My religion or my God is the only and most superior God; therefore, you are without the thread of universality that connects us all and need to be cast aside and condemned for binding with an inferior or dangerous group or faith. We are unequally yoked; therefore, we are too unequal on a religious level to coexist. We can never function as equals, mate, date, or rear children. My commitment and allegiance on the religious level requires not only that I not entertain the possibility of the existence of another equally relevant and valid faith, but that I condemn or minimize any that do, even if I have known them and have accepted them as my brothers or neighbors for years. My school of thought and neighbors of concern are within my group and all outsiders and their views are looked at with disdain.

My words will profess love and concern for all, but you will know me by my actions, which will always come from the religious level and not the deeper spiritual level. I will recognize and claim you as my own when you convert and come out of the world or the darkness. Christianity: "Love your neighbor as you love your-self." Taoism: "Regard your neighbor's gain as your own gain, and your neighbor's loss as your own loss." And who is our neighbor? It is not the guy across the aisle or across the street, but anyone in need. That which bind and restrain under the banner of man-created titles, entities, and institutions have served a man-directed purpose and agenda very well for centuries.

It should not be difficult to see why we are still having trouble throughout the land when centuries of mankind's teaching and preaching have only amounted to partial unity under the best organized religious banners. Centuries of disputes within united entities and opposing entities have been at the human or religious level and have accounted for sanctioned human atrocities in the millions. This has included countless tortures, human sacrifices, decapitations, burnings at the stake, entombments, and any mayhem that could be imagined. The levels of where humans would go and have gone to prove their commitment to their faith have served to cement the importance and value of these men-created faiths while convoluting and diluting the value at that deeper spiritual level.

The one God, one Life, and that Universality or Spirituality of mankind as purported by the Golden Rule has been usurped. Many have promoted and profited from the manipulation and exploitation of the perceived differences between entities and the perceived differences within entities. Sometimes the religious differences within some groupings keep fellow worshippers from fellowshipping outside their gathering, and although both proclaim the love of God, it is not deep enough (spirited) to overcome their dislike for each other. Playing up to the good graces of the religious institution or its hierarchy assumes spiritual significance; however, they are not one and the same, so spirituality is displaced by religion. This is done on such a grand scale and in such a subtle and polished manner across various religions that the believability of the previous statement is easily trumped by assumed creditability, so the lie prevails. This has contributed to centuries of man's failure in understanding and applying the Golden Rule. However, it may be in sync with the script of that other Golden Rule: He who has the gold, makes the rule. Maybe it's the Green Rule that binds us, or is it that it blinds us?

# Field of Dreams

My father thought that if you ever got off your knees you were ready for some type of fieldwork. If you stopped crawling and stood up, he would say, "Take him to the cucumber field tomorrow." Remember, his home rule existed everywhere and any adult could tell you what to do. He didn't even have to know the adult. I could say a new man from China came to the field today, and he would say, "Did you do what he told you?" "No sir, I did not understand what he said." "That don't matter, boy, you better do what he tells you." "Yes sir" would be the next answer. My father died thinking the storekeeper who my brother Lenwood and I mistakenly took ten dollars of gas from should have "gotten hold to us" and taken at least nine dollars out of our behinds. He used to quote "Spare the rod and spoil the child" like he made it up. He thought the only thing more useful than a stick was a log.

As a young boy I spent much of my summers in the field with three or four other families. I don't ever remember him saying to my siblings or me that he gave Mrs. Monroe, who was often the only adult in the fields with us, permission to discipline us. It was a pervasive case of assumed authority. I don't remember her telling me she ever asked for permission or that she was granted permission. It was like a birthright or neighborhood watch gone awry that found its way straight to her, and there was nothing I could do about it. Let me just conclude by saying: Without permission, Mrs. Monroe was able to exact remission and total submission toward fulfilling her dutiful mission to rid me of harmful emissions.

# Criminal Interest or Criminal Intent?

The recent housing crisis has put many upside down in what was once considered most individuals' best investment. It's almost as if they have thrown away their money, an insult once reserved for renters. How many homeowners really understand how mortgage amortization works as it relates to interest and principal? As monthly contributions are made to the interest and principal category per the loan agreement, I have always wondered about the authentic interest of the homeowner.

I have been baffled by conversations with bankers, mortgage brokers, and real estate professionals who are entangled in negative amortization loans for themselves. Who among us should better understand the real estate terms and lingo than those who have chosen it as an occupation? There are so many different rates, terms, and clauses that can affect value and equity that the average homeowners just sign whatever is shoved in front of them. It just seems to be a fertile ground for knavery, equity grabbing, and predatory lending.

From the onset, the manner in which mortgage loans are computed disgraces a Truth In Lending Disclosure Statement. A $325,000 loan at 5% fixed for thirty years calculates into a monthly payment of $1,744.67, which includes an interest payment of $1,354.17 and a principal amount of $390.50. That translates into 78% for the bank's interest and 22% for the homeowner's interest. Now imagine that same loan at 10%, which, by the way, I would have been happy to find in the runaway interest rate days of the early '80s. I was tickled pink when I secured a home loan at 13.5% interest in 1983. Anyway, this same loan would now have a monthly payment of $2,852.11 with an interest amount of $2,708.33 and a principal total of $143.77. That is 95% for the bank's interest and 5% for the homeowner's interest. I may be able to get a better deal from a loan shark.

If I could get body parts omitted as collateral it probably would be a better route. Subtract $143.77 from $325,000 for a balance of $324,856.23, multiply the interest rate 10% by 1/12th of the loan balance of the previous month and the homeowner gets to add $1.20 more to his side of the equation over what was posted the last month and the bank gets to tack on $2,707.14 to its side. The homeowner is well on his way to repaying his loan. He just has 358 months to go. It is hard to keep our kids in school for 360 minutes. Our high school seniors are dropping out with 360 days left and marriages are falling apart in less than 360 days, and we are surprised that people are walking away from 360-month commitments that have been debased by the very institutions and policymakers most responsible for diluting an already convoluted arrangement of its value.

A homeowner's partnership with a banking establishment that rewards the banking partner with up to 95% or more to a homeowner's 5% or less is outrageous. The banking partner also holds a demand clause so even after over 180 payments (½) are satisfied to the tune of $513,500, which is approximately 1.58% of the original loan, the bank could call the loan due for a number of reasons. If the homeowner defaults at this point, the banking partner gets to keep his $453,789.20 that has been paid in interest along with the homeowner's $59,590.17 paid to the principal and any other additional equity that may have accumulated. In addition, the banker gets the house back, since it was secured by the mortgage. If there is any outstanding balance after the dust settles, the bank gets to recoup that also from the homeowner.

It is a legal ass-whipping that would be very hard to match by even the most ruthless gangbangers. To add insult to injury, the banker has no restrictions on who he can sell the property to outside of direct connections to the bank. He could sell it to the person next door even if that person was the one deemed responsible for the homeowner losing his home or the whole economic meltdown. You see, none of those most likely responsible for this crisis got any jail time so they are all free to benefit from this in any manner they choose. The homeowner could have been the most law-abiding citizen in town, followed the script as it was set up, the so-called easy payment plan, only to learn in the end that he never had an interest that he controlled, even though he is the one who made all the contributions to the principal side and the interest side.

The "due on sale clause" would forbid a transfer even if he could have found someone to take over the loan. A short sale would require agreement from the bank and any subordinate parties, and even if successful, it would leave a smear on the homeowner's credit report. The whole interest and principal arrangement of debt repayment (amortization) linked to a tax break inducement is shrouded in a funny math that bars any true interest for the homeowner. Since education/school loans are set up in a similar fashion, a double jeopardy of interest duping gives these arrangements a definite element of criminal interest. The only other question remaining would be, is it criminal intent?

# Invest in Those Who Invest in You

All purchases have an associated labor cost that can be measured by the time expended to acquire that product. Is the trade-off in labor time equal to or greater than the loss of time to what would have been gained from the growth in human interaction? Time spent apart, once lost, is lost forever, so if the exchange of that time amounts to trivial accomplishments or pseudo gains, we have created an equation for a negative return on that investment.

I was reminded of how far man can be off the mark in assigned value and the twisted meaning of work (labor) just by watching one documentary. It was a re-creation of an incident where a young man with a partner parked outside as a lookout or getaway driver; whatever the case, he was a willing participant. The other young man breaks into the home of a jewelry storeowner. Finding only the grandmother there, he makes a decision that she has lived long enough, so he kills her. Three younger children, ages twelve, nine, and six, came home from school. Of course, additional schooling is probably what both of these young men could have used. One of the assailants forced one of the children, at gunpoint, to call the father at work and report an emergency at home that required his attendance.

When the father got home, the assailant forced him to unlock a jewelry safe and took the contents. He killed the father and the three children, execution style. I am not sure how much his accomplice participated in the actual shootings but, either way, this was their work for the day. So for maybe two hours of labor they obtained some bling, which, to them, had a greater value than the five lives they traded for it.

To get an even deeper understanding of how far off the mark we can be on what we think is valuable, the main assailant actually thought he had done something that would make an uncle proud. This uncle he admired was a high-level gangster. The assailant's assignment of value to the ways and accomplishments of the gangster life led him to conclude he could go to work in a similar fashion and instantly be somebody in a world that he had identified as having the "somebodies" who were important to him. The shame of this is the uncle's example, as the nephew understood it, probably contributed to providing some of the motivation for this tragedy. The uncle's disapproval of the action was so sharp that it forced a dismantling of his entire life, yet the disapproval came as a shock to the nephew.

This case typified an extreme case of misplaced values and an extreme faulty investment of time. On a lower and far less extreme level, we choose to trade our hourly wages in exchange for things that often yield less valuable and sometime negative dividends more often than we realize. A case in point is when a mother who is employed at $20 per hour for forty hours a week ($800 per week) pays for a twenty-year-old son's apartment at $600 per month and his car at $200 per month. This is a labor cost to her of forty hours per month. One week of labor ($800) is being invested in him, yet in return for her investment of time (forty hours), she gets almost nothing and even has to force a phone conversation longer than five minutes unless he needs more of her labor (money). The mother has to work a part-time job (twenty hours at $10) to make up for her lost wages, which also decrease the investment of time available for her teenage daughter. Yet, the son refuses to go to school for eight hours a month at the mother's request in exchange for her committing up to sixty hours a month on his behalf.

When money does come through the young adult's hand, it never occurs to him to share any of his windfall with his mother. Instead, he will buy new videos, games, etc. (invest in someone else's business that does not invest in him) and spend or invest his time in sharing with his friends who are unable or unwilling to assist him when he has an unfunded need. The investment of resources in the man who owns the video franchise business instead of investing his windfall with the mother who invests in him makes that a negative exchange investment for the child and the mother. By choosing to spend (invest) time with marginal and pseudo friends instead of the mother, the reduction in reserves of the mother-son relationship amounts to a loss in human factors (love/sharing) that cannot be passed to the next generation.

The multiplication of this process of negative trading and exchange in different scenarios throughout the country and world has amounted to an extremely poor balance sheet, especially in the minority communities. Our most valuable commodities have always been each other, but in our quest to improve our status through the use of trumped-up mediums and supplies, we have become awash in hype and lost to the degree that our investment in time, labor, energy, and resources have become mired in worthless, shallow, overvalued, and unsubstantiated exchanges that have amounted to negative accounts and a declining reserve in human and monetary capital.

Our misunderstanding and misapplication of this investment principle have made wastelands of our homes and communities where everyone has been weakened by this trumped-up value of the gangster life that contributes nothing (bling, etc.) in exchange for what they take out (safety and security). It isn't a stretch to see how the exchange of a life for what the gangster considers valuable assures that the balance sheet will always be in the red. If our most valuable commodities are each other, then our investment portfolio—which includes shooting, maiming, and killing each other—are examples of how we are destroying and burning money yet somehow expecting a return on the ashes. We honor the ashes with tattoos, toasts, and Facebook highlights. It is a sad, sordid, and useless commentary that is identified, submitted, and accepted as a meaningful tribute, trade-off, or exchange for our greatest investment: each other.

# A Deeper Inheritance

As I rise mounted firmly on the shoulders of many generations, I have thought often about those lessons with which I have been entrusted. Everyone leaves something in life whether he wants to or not. The true measure of what one leaves as their entrustment is determined by the value of its enrichment to others, not in purse, but in the human spirit for generations to come. There is nothing about the abundance of things that contributes to the advancement of human interests; in fact, the desire and worship of such accolades restrains and defines development in a way that precludes it from recognizing and appreciating life in its purest form.

It seems we have lost the ability to extract pleasure from simplicity. An inheritance not heavily latent with spoils and pricey ornaments is considered unworthy and a disgrace. It doesn't take in account the blood, sweat, and tears expended to leave it. In reality, a sweat equity gift that does not include a lesson in sweat diminishes both the giver and the receiver.

A perfect example of this is derived from a house I purchased about ten miles from Myrtle Beach, South Carolina. I later learned this house was a gift, free and clear, from a grandmother who lost her legs to diabetes. She bypassed her children and bequeathed it to her granddaughter. Her granddaughter collected the physical assets of her grandmother's gift and then paid an empty homage to her grandmother's sacrifice by losing it in just over two years. How the granddaughter handled the spoils of her monetary inheritance without the benefit and understanding of the sacrifice, hard work, suffering, and discipline required to bring that gift to fruition only validated the granddaughter's misunderstanding of its intrinsic value and her obligations to the generations behind her as entrusted to her by her grandmother.

# To Sir With Love: Giving Honor To My Uncle

There is much made about the parental influence on children and how parents' modeling and role playing have more to do with outcomes than what parents say to their children. In many respects, that is probably true and safe to say.

Then there is peer influence. We all know how awesome or devastating the influence of one peer or peer group can be; hence, efforts to monitor and control that to a desired affect has been a staple in many households. With all of this known, it is hard to believe that sometimes the greatest influence on a child may be someone they latch onto for some reason that may be completely unknown to the parent and sometimes even the child until years later.

I thought about this recently as I was reflecting on the influences in my own life. I think sometimes we do not think very deep about this matter, and when we do, we look at the obvious—parents, siblings, educators, religious leaders—and we leave it there. That can be a mistake of a singular proportion when we are talking about one person, but imagine how grand an error it might be when we multiply that one person by the millions.

In my case, of course, I had the usual influence of family, friends, school, and religious establishments but for years I did not think much about an extended influence beyond that which I came in contact with every day. I certainly did not give much thought to the possibility of someone I only saw once every two or three years as having any significant level of influence in my life, not until recently. His name was E.G. Brown. I had the honor of being able to care for him in the latter years of his life, and it was during that time that I learned the impact he had on me, my thinking, and my decision making throughout my life.

Whenever I saw him, I always thought he presented himself in such an impressive manner that I wanted to emulate him. I would hear him talk to my father and other adults in the community about real estate and business opportunities at such a grand level that it would be viewed as foolhardy by most of them. Of course, I did not understand any of it either, but I did want the pocket full of change and goods he appeared to always have for his family and the many families in our neighborhood, including ours, of which he shared. Sometimes he had countless outfits either two sizes too large, odd-colored and mismatched shoes, but we were very happy to get them.

I caught him one time sneaking some money to my mother, which is probably a route he used on numerous occasions for to do so in any other manner was an affront to my father and perhaps the other men in the community. He was a family man first and, of course, a businessman of some means, not extravagant or boastful. He was caring, very humble, and willing to share his time, finances, and most importantly, his intellect and wisdom in the ways of the world.

When we normally think of influences, I don't think we naturally zero in on figures who appear to represent fringes of our lives. In my case, I have been able to recognize and document how that perhaps was an error on my part. I guess such a figure could wield a tremendous amount of power, good or bad, in the lives of others without ever knowing it or having to be as accountable as parents, schools, or other entities. I am not unmindful of the fact that I may represent that figure to many. My hope is that I may carry the banner of my uncle with the same dignity and class with which he carried it.

# Hijacked

We seem to hear a lot today about various individuals and groups hijacking religions and using them for their own purpose and agenda. "Hijacking" literally means to commandeer, seize, or take over. It does not have to be by force, and it does not have to be an object or thing; it could be an idea. On the subject of religion, it may seem a little uncanny for me to refer to institutionalize religion as religion hijacked. I will state some arguments to support that later but, for now, I want to discuss subversive as a concept and as the ideological route to most religious inclusion.

Hijacking may be the means or method most useful in facilitating inclusion. Subversive ideology and subversive individuals and groups have always been at the origin of all religions as best I can tell. For that not to have been the case, there would have been instant agreement on every issue at the formation of the first religion. Certain high-profile subversive groups such as the Taliban and Al-Qaeda are sometimes presented as anomalies of historic proportion when, in fact, almost every major religion at one point, including Christianity, has found itself so opposed to the status quo that its survival meant it had to go underground. Even within Christianity today, such sects as Jehovah's Witnesses and Mormons are viewed by some as not mainstream, and even such nonreligious groups as the Masons, are believed to be dissident to some religious ideology.

Since humans are unable to live two or three millennium, once very hot topics like the Spanish Inquisition and Luther's 95 Theses that are no longer a part of our current vernacular become insignificant and irrelevant when factored against today's concerns. Imbedded political, social, and religious ideology slanted against justice often requires subversive operations to bring force on that injustice.

If such issues persist from a distant era, the change in demographics may warrant a change in subversive tactics and ideology. The plight and fight for recognition of all types of groups and ideology have been the same from era to era. One individual or group has the power, control, and decision-making ability, and the other individuals or groups want or believe they should have it, or at least a share of it, and are willing to resort to any means necessary to get it, while the other individual or group fights to maintain or extend control. Hence, subversive is the label that is put on groups outside the mainstream until they assimilate, then they become part of the mainstream that fight to keep upstarts out.

Though subversive individual or group ideology and tactics may be viewed by some as hijacking, it is not always synonymous with bad. Apartheid, a system of legal racial segregation and exploitation, represented the mainstream of South Africa from 1948 to 1994, and Umkhonto We Sizwe, the armed wing of the ANC (African National Congress), represented a subversive group that helped pave the way for South Africa's Nelson Mandela's release from prison and later his presidency from 1994–1999.

So how has institutionalized religion hijacked religion? It is very easy to understand how some fringe group with a separate agenda from the body of a religion may use its ideology to forge a different direction than the majority in the mainstream would find acceptable. When religion is capitalized and institutionalized by the mainstream, its sacredness and sometimes the religion itself is hijacked by a tactic called normalization. Under the cover of this subtle and innocent-appearing course of action, it is not viewed as hijacking because the commandeering is done with the illusion of the full cooperation of the masses that collaborate and reinforce the illusion. Once inclusion is synchronized, seldom are views advanced that are detached from the masses as indicated by this comment: "I like your Christ. I do not like your Christians. Your Christians are so unlike your Christ" (Mohandas Gandhi). So, normalization begets a script for the masses. Most individuals I know depend on religious leaders to provide them with spiritual guidance.

After a person determines where he is going to live and whom he is going to live with, he turns to an institutional-approved spiritual authority to assist and guide him; this inspired person, who is no less and no greater than himself, under the auspices of a sanctioned institution or title, has unknowingly or knowingly hijacked spirituality with the application of normalcy. The spiritual leader becomes the conduit to the conduit of salvation. The individual must yield and conform to specific instructions known best by the chosen representative of God.

These instructions may include how often the individual should attend religious gatherings, what garments should be worn, what to eat, what duties should be included in the gathering and outside the gathering, and how often the individual must pray and even in what direction he must pray. By subtly yet firmly urging whom to live for in this life and in the afterlife, a complete takeover is orchestrated; it is a hijacking. It will also require a percentage of the person's income and a generous amount of the individual's time to complete this hijacking. Resisting or abstaining is almost synonymous with blasphemy. It is, after all, God's money and God's time. It is very difficult to buck the norm, especially if God is on the side of the norm. Once the norm becomes an established custom, it is only a small step to get the law to cover and enforce it.

If there is not a separation of state and religion, then the law can exact extreme punishment for nonconformance to the norm, all under the name of God. It sounds a little like the goal of other subversive groups that have yet to be normalized, since they are starting with stressing God as the justification for their actions and the need to yield to this higher authority to achieve this more purposeful life that all religions promise. The knowledge that what is being done for you can be done by you is strategically omitted. In fact, the representative of God may be a hindrance to your spirituality because he represents an institution and its by-laws before God . . . before you.

If you take away the accreditation, tax-exemption status, community standing, and, oh yeah, the money, and put those benefits in another institution, you may witness an exodus to another institution more worthy of being hijacked. Now, of course, this is not applicable to all God's representatives, but it is the hue of more than a few.

# When Helping Hurts

This may sound like a paradox but, in this day and time, it is too common to be viewed as such. Governments do it, individuals do it, and organizations do it also. So if they are supposed to help and are trying to help, why are they hurting the ones they should be helping? If I interject that it is complicated, maybe I should also counter that either you are helping or hurting; it's like black or white, day or night—can't get any simpler than that. Besides, at least in the government and some organizations' cases, they have policies in place to make sure money and resources are used to help people and not hurt them, right? Change the policy if you are not getting the desired results. What's so complicated about that?

There is something about human nature or human conditioning that fosters a need for help, and there is something about the same human nature or human conditioning that fosters a need to want to help. As help arrives and is accepted, there is something about that same human nature or conditioning that acquires expectancy in permanence that is not shared by the human nature or human conditioning of the helper or giver. How the helper thinks, feels, or believes about the permanence of the giving doesn't matter to the one being helped. In fact, even if the status of the giver changes, where the giver is no longer able to give as it once gave, that makes little difference to the expectancy of the receiver.

Making that a part of the large print before the first help is given is not a relevant point to the receiver of the gift. In fact, remaining in the status of having a need is so integral to qualifying for help that it becomes the built-in "how" in getting all needs met. A status of anything and everything that is synonymous with helpless or victim must be maintained at all costs by the one being helped. A permanent need is more important than the permanent capacity to give. It essentially means that if the giver no longer has the means to give, then the giver made false pledges and should not have offered to help in the first place, especially if the help amounted to a paltry amount according to the one being helped. The helped level of expectancy was created by the helper and since the helper can no longer follow through at that level of expectancy, then the helper is guilty of malfeasance and now must help even against the helper's will or be subject to criminal action. Now the ones who chose to help are guilty of violating the rights of the ones who received help for curtailing or eliminating the help.

In a sense, the helped has carved out a no-fault, no-responsibility, and no-accountability position that borders on pathological. Medication should affirm a need for help and reinforce its permanency. The need for help is now certifiable. There is no benefit in improving beyond the point of needing help.

Once help is no longer a part of the assistance and support that is still strengthening a participant in an active and growing process, it has outlived its usefulness and is now a part of the hurt. The ones receiving the help must stay engaged with their help and utilize only what is necessary to help elevate their situation to the next level. If more help becomes necessary, then the quantity and quality of the help is reviewed only after the effort of the one who is being helped is reviewed thoroughly for his contribution to self-sufficiency. Ownership of outcomes must stay in the hands of the one being helped. All efforts by the helped to take their hands off their situation must be quelled. If the helper assumes more of a role than assistant and is doing more work than the one being helped, then the helper has now become a hurter and must be sequestered from the process. Again, if the ownership shift is allowed, then the failure of the helped is blame on the helper by the helped and the helped absolve themselves of all responsibilities and claim now to be in need of additional help, this time not due to their own action, but as a result of poor and inadequate help by the helper. The helped can repeat this process over and over until creditability of a need for help appears justifiable.

This is a learned and practiced behavior on how to get needs met that is reinforced and rewarded by the offerings of the givers.

Unfortunately, the giver's and the receiver's definition and understanding of help are dissonances. Excuse me; it is unfortunate for the giver. To the receiver or helped, ignorance of the process is no excuse to discontinue giving. To the giver or helper, you must conclude there are some people who can't be helped, at least by their definition and understanding of help. Maybe it is a paradox; helping hurts the helper.

# A Person of More Than Interest

When one of my duties in the prison system was that of a case manager, inmates would find it dutiful on their part to educate me about their rights and how the system works, and, of course, why they were wrongfully convicted. They generally believed strongly in "innocent until proven guilty," but advised me that this was the tenet in the law that was most often violated by "us"—those of us who represented the justice system, and that surely included us prison officials. In fact, we were the worst of the bunch because we participated in keeping innocent people behind bars. Be that as it may, the main issue was that even though the law always said innocent until proven guilty, the prevailing feeling by most inmates I conferred with indicated that was a bunch of crock, and that they were guilty until proven innocent.

The assumption of innocence never applied to them. When I would ask if they ever committed a crime of which they were not convicted (because I know I have even if it was stealing a piece of candy), their answer would be, "Certainly." I would say, in those cases, "all of us" have received the benefit of the presumption of innocence because in those cases, we are certainly not being presumed as guilty, even though the facts clearly indicate we are guilty. They would say, "Those cases do not count because I never had my day in court to prove my innocence." I would say, "You just told me you committed the crime but did not get caught." Well, they would say that, "In those cases, you could say I was a person of interest, but I am still supposed to be innocent until proven guilty, and since that has not been proven by a court of law, those cases have nothing to do with anyone presuming I am innocent; they just did not catch me." Then I would say, "Listen, person of interest, if you are responsible for two bodies buried in a dense forest, your day in court or your presumption of innocence has nothing to do with your innocence. Proven by a court of law of your innocence cannot make you innocent if you are, in fact, the person responsible for those two people lying in the woods. A presumption of innocence for you, in this case, is as useless as a presumption of life for the two dead people left in the woods."

Proof has nothing to do with innocence or guilt. We are only innocent if we did not commit the crime, and to argue that our law always assumes you are guilty, if that was the case, would be just as fair to the victim as assuming an assailant is innocent. To assume a benefit where none is due conjures up the old saying of what "assume" means about you and me. In many cases, innocence and guilt from our day in court have more to do with the quality of representation and the quality of information gathering than the reality of the case.

Innocent men have been proven guilty, and guilty men have been proven innocent, and the presumption or assumption, either way, is immaterial to the truth if the truth is never uncovered and remains buried in the woods. A man, in this case, exonerated by a court of law after a presumption of innocence, may dance for years through the woods over his dead bodies and proclaim his innocence to the world, but he is not innocent and never was innocent, even when the law presumes he was innocent.

In more than a few cases, I have talked to inmates who can relate to this scenario, and the one truth that was consistent is that anyone found innocent by a court of law actually believed they were made innocent and talked highly about how the system worked so beautifully in that case and felt no hint of guilt, even when they knew it to be otherwise. After such a beautiful day in court, to even continue referring to him as a person of interest was slanderous and a violation of the rights of an innocent man—a complete mockery. A person who is, in fact, guilty is certainly more than a person of interest, regardless of what our courts have determined.

# The Relationship Value

When it comes to sex, money, and relationship, the most valuable of this trio should be relationship. Relationships, however, are often ruined by money or sex and not necessarily in that order.

Consider, for instance, how a relationship can become tainted when sex or money—and especially sex for money—enters the equation. Money entanglements all too frequently tend to diminish the human value of the individual, whether it's an arranged marriage to a stranger or hiring a high-priced call girl as a business date. When money is used to initiate a relationship or as the glue to hold a relationship together, it is unlikely the relationship will have any long-term value. This is not an area where class rules, because wealthy and poor people alike may value money over relationships and see money as more dependable even when it comes to marital sex or long-term relationships.

For those that say, "Don't mess with my money," they are declaring what's valuable to them because they generally don't make any distinction to wife, husband, child, minister, or any other relationship. I have also often heard, "Don't lend a friend money if you want to keep that friend." As much as I don't want to believe that, I have seen it shaken out to be true too often to ignore the truth in it. People have lost longstanding childhood relationships and other close friendships over loans. The sad part of that is the dollar amount of the loan may be a single digit.

Generations of family members have been caught up in money issues and the relationships in the family are written off. Sometime the ones that owe are the angriest and the ones insisting on ending the relationship and declaring the other as doing them wrong. They get mad at people about asking them about their money. Not only have some killed relationships because of money, some have even killed one another because of money. Again, the actual sums involved are paltry. In many of these cases, combatants like to offer the principle as the reason for the killing and yet clearly the relationship had little value if an unwritten and newly stated rule trumped a valued life,

When it comes to sex, women tend to believe sex is a thing that men will do anything for. Although they expect not to be referred to as a "thing," they generally believe their thing has greater value than whatever thing the male has to offer. Therefore, they must receive additional goodies for their thing in order to not come up short in the relationship department. Men rarely think they should receive bonuses for their sex thing in a relationship with women; however, they generally think the woman should maintain whatever level of sexual accommodations was agreed upon at the outset of the relationship throughout its duration. If she doesn't, he usually believes she has reneged and has made sex a pawn in the relationship regardless of what else has occurred between them.

The man sees sex as an entitlement or duty in the relationship and separate from other functions and activities of the relationship. The woman, on the other hand, sees sex as a part of everything, her personhood and her livelihood, exclusively hers, to be used as she chooses and not belonging to the relationship, except as defined by her. While such interactions require the agreement of two people, she believes the man's position is a given but that her agreement requires satisfaction of certain strings which are subject to change depending on his behavior and other factors debatably within his control. She may not say sex is a pawn but she certainly may think of it as her best leverage against any other dissatisfaction she has with him or with the running of the household.

She may also feel that if she is putting out and he is coming up short in any area of household affairs, he must up his game and bring more to the table in order for her to keep putting out. That usually means dishing out more money, providing more things, doing more chores, or a combination thereof. This amounts to bonuses if her demands are baseless, or if it is due to her unequal monetary assignment of the value of her sex. Her sex and his sex are a part of the total sex that is under her control. It is generally treated as she treats all money. Her money is her money and his money is her money. No real man will have a problem with that. It is, after all, in sync with, "A happy wife makes a happy life."

Sex is never detached from other occurrences and activities in the relationship. A wrong word or misstatement by the man may get rolled into silent treatment, mood swings, and ultimately a just cause for no sex, so called "shutting it down," as only she can proclaim. If he doesn't want a sex interruption, he needs to stay correct. She is the one doing the giving and he is the one getting or receiving. It is not reciprocal or mutual and for him to think of it that way means he got it twisted. If a man is not willing to do something extra, as stated earlier, she is getting the short end of the stick. "What is he doing for me?" she asks. If he mumbles, "The same thing you are doing for me," cold showers or couch slumbers have been known to follow.

It may be perfectly all right for her to insert sex as a bargaining chip for more things or more money, but the moment the man suggests more sex for contributing more, he will be accused of treating her like a prostitute. Says the woman, "He is not going to have sex with me and treat me any kind of way." He should not treat you any kind of way because of how much he loves and cares about you as a person. The emphasis should be on the relationship. Some believe they should have things done for them with the hint of sex. They believe the man should put out because he is being graced by her presence and beauty. These relationships fall apart when someone feels cheated, either because the man is not putting out enough or the woman's sex is insufficient to what the man believes he should be getting. Both believe they are being shortchanged and because the relationship was never more valuable than the sex, the relationship without the sex loses its steam.

Both male and female used sex and valued sex differently but both placed more value on sex than they did each other. The female used sex for the perks and comforts and the male monitored and gauged the cost of the perks and comforts against the amount of sex he was receiving. The man generally grows to resent the female for stiffing him for sex and the female generally grows to resent the male for treating her as if she was cheap. When sex is no longer working for them, they have no use for each other, so the relationship that was nothing more than a sex relationship, must collapse.

When having sex or not having sex defines, changes, or damages the state of the relationship, it is a good chance that sex carried more significance than caring for one another. Procreation and STD'S often become an afterthought in this sex-crazed environment of displaced values; hence, this diluted and once cherished arrangement becomes valueless. What is left is anger and bitterness—emotions foreign to love. If children are outcomes of these arrangements, they will almost certainly experience some discomfort from these relationships of misplaced affections.

# The Relationship Value II

The value of relationships cannot be overemphasized and, thus, merits a second essay on the subject.

The true emphasis on relationships gives our existence value and elevates us above the instinctive and primitive interaction that defines many of the other species. It explains our total commitment and sacrifice of life and limb when these essential bonds are threatened. It is an authentic and true connection with a person that activates our tear ducts and jerks our deepest emotions from some of the most remote areas of the world even when we have never personally touched or seen the person. Whether it is the death of a pop idol or reading about the senseless murder of innocent children and teachers at Sandy Hook Elementary School in Connecticut, it is that damage to the relationship piece that spurs these radical and universal emotions in us. It is not the death that moves us to cry, but the death of the bond that we had with that person. If that were not the case, we would be an emotional wreck—crying and falling apart all the time—because people die every minute all over the world. It is the relationship that stops a crazed criminal from continuing a killing spree when he hears the voice of his mother, or that halts a serial rapist in his tracks when he recognizes the victim as his sister.

Relationships are so significant that they are universally assigned, and though we are able to make occasional adjustment to friendships, those adjustments have to be made within the constraints of our era of assignment. We can't dismiss a current relationship of value and replace it with another relationship from someone from the Mesopotamia period. As for kinships, they are also relationships of destiny, foretold and assigned intentionally as a part of a greater purpose, outside our pay grade or area of authority. Our passing and connections in time are not accidents. How we ascribe value to these relationships should be with respect to that eternal truth.

Relationships connect us in a way that nothing else in the world can. There is an insatiable desire to connect. On the other hand, it is our inadequate and improper nourishment of the relationship piece that foster gang expansions, nation destabilization, and unrest in our communities and homes.

The misplaced assignment of the value of relationships allows the interjection of the "N" word and "B" word into our psyche as a part of a cultural phenomenon that redefines, reduces, and in some cases, decimates the quality of how we relate to each other. Those that try to upgrade or reclassify these references as terms of endearments are well-meaning individuals using flawed and vain attempts of positive spinning on something intrinsically defective. Because the true value of relationships is misunderstood and misguided by even well-meaning individuals, many others, with no clue, trample relationships over and over without ever understanding its vital effect on their happiness.

When the value of relationships has been ignored, human suffering has flourished. When we relate to each other at a lower level or at any level that signifies little or no value, we are capable of committing any number of atrocities to each other, even to old women and children, without feeling anything. When our minds can conclude that a species that possess all the natural features as ourselves, are subhuman—such as Germen were able to do with the Jews during World War II, or as the early settlers of America were able to do with those of African descent—we are capable of putting every conceivable option of inhumanity on the table. It creates a situation not much different from stomping a roach. We generally share no relationship of value with a roach's family; therefore, we will not shed any tears or feel anything about the roach's loss.

Barring any mental health disorder that may preclude a person from experiencing a normal range of emotion from the human relationship experience, the true value of the relationship at its highest level of connectivity will hold us accountable to each other. Our pains and joys for each other are shared as if they are ours and the manner in which we treat that relationship speaks volumes about the level of our human connectivity, or the level of our human disconnection, with respect to our Maker.

# Life

Life is a series of constantly moving events. Any time man is tripped up, stumbles, or gets stuck, the constantly moving events do not slow up or go to check on him; they leave him behind. The damage mounts based on the factor rating of the event, which includes the magnitude of the stumble and the length of the slow-down or downtime. The number of events in a day, week, month, or year that breaks your stride become factors in your elevation or dissension and determines your destination.

Although there are some who think of themselves as event movers and shakers, the events I am referring to are unaffected by these movers and shakers and count them among their subjects. We are all subject to these events of life. The unfortunate part is that even though all are affected and all have an equal chance of being affected, not all are affected equally.

The events that trip or stick some are pebbles to others, and some are able to keep rolling over boulders. Figuring out how to be a boulder crusher does not change the events of life, but it can change the life of the person subjected to the events.

# Success Is . . . ?

A man drives onto the field of a crowded football stadium to give a speech on success. He is driving a 1977 Chevrolet Vega. It has several dents and a two-tone paint job. It is smoking and leaking gas and oil on the football turf. It looks like it has been wrecked or pulled out from under water and that perhaps another collision at a precise angle might straighten it out some and improve its value. The crowd is stunned. When he gets out, he has to roll his window down to open the outside lock to let himself out. His clothing looks like he slept in it for a week, and a closer peek indicates he may even be a little too friendly with the bottle.

As he starts to speak, he rambles and uses broken English. When the crowd cannot take it anymore, they boo and leave the stadium. It is cleared in less than thirty minutes. One homeless man stays behind partly because he sleeps beneath the stadium, and partly to offer this wretched soul a place to sleep tonight. As he walks up to the podium, the man slowly removes his disguises and introduces himself as Bill Gates, and he proceeds to give him the best speech he ever heard about success. Now, of course, this is not true.

I think most of us have heard not to judge a book by its cover, and some have actually lived long enough to see the wisdom in that statement. What we see belies success. Success is more about what we feel than what we see. Yet, when it comes to what constitutes success in life, we seem to be awash in riches, accolades, titles, and other outer trappings.

Money seems to be the most universal determinant of success. A man pulling down twenty million dollars a year who can't pay his bills is as broke and as unsuccessful—if money is a criterion—as a man making twenty thousand dollars a year who can't pay his bills; he's just broke at a higher level. Money as an indication of success seems to have been reinforced by rapper/artist/philanthropist 50 Cent's 2005 movie, which

I translated into Get Rich or Go to Jail Tryin' or maybe Get Rich or Go to Hell Tryin'. Through all the inferences and hoopla, there appears to be an orchestrated attempt to treat money and success as synonyms. The nearly one hundred and twenty million dollar auction of Edvard Munch's The Scream in May 2012 is an even higher example of how success can be separated into the mega-successful.

Success is individually defined and means different things to different people, yet failure is the same for everyone; specifically, the inability to accomplish one's goal, whatever that goal may be. Success is a feeling of accomplishment, different from individual to individual, yet for all, it is an entrustment filled with thankfulness, humility, and responsibility. It is more felt than it is seen or heard. Unlike The Scream, it is silent and it speaks for itself. The vehicle Mr. Gates drove up in was made up. It had no dents and was in pristine condition. The oil and gas it seeped were not real. All the mechanical parts such as internal door handles worked wonderfully. And, of course, Mr. Gates was not drunk. At the completion of his speech, Mr. Gates presented the homeless man with the museum Vega. You see, it was the very last Vega ever produced and was worth well over a million dollars, proving, once again, that you cannot judge a book—or success—by its cover.

# Conclusion

In my book, In the Shadow of Sacrifice, I share a lot about my father in the stories and contributions he gave to my siblings, the community, and me. I am the beneficiary and trustee of what I believe is the greatest inheritance in the world, and most of that came from my mother. I say that with the deepest respect and regard for my father. My mother had a quiet strength and deep love for life that lured me into feelings of peace and serenity. She was poised, courteous, and dignified. She had a hearing impairment, yet she had a deep and broad understanding of the value and the significance of factors concerning the progression and security of her family. My mother was able to instantly and consistently tease out trivialities, gossip, and her personal interests and aspirations when it came to the concerns of her family.

There are many who would put forth the position that my mother should have left my father years ago and not suffered the degradation, womanizing, and abuse she endured. A deeper look at the times, options, resources, and possibilities reveals an insight into her thinking that constitutes the ultimate sacrifice of which I and my siblings directly benefited. To lose oneself in the service of others is sacrifice taken the extra mile. My mother knew my father was a much better father and provider than he was a husband; to that end and how that would benefit her children is what drove her. She knew he cared more about his children than any other agent or avenue available to her at the time or any time she could foresee. The mere number of us meant she would take a chance at auctioning us off in many different directions and that, to her, was a greater evil than what she was enduring. She was a constant and, in her quiet way, a formidable barrier. It was my mother who kept us together.

My mother's sacrifice as a military wife early in her marriage is not a part of my story, yet it should not be overlooked, but chronicled as her sacrifice is tallied. My father provided the monetary support but she would pay a greater price in living with him, and her children would be her solace. Time has all but eliminated that seemingly coerced choice. Yet, time has not eroded its value; it has validated it. In fact, I believe it is the wanton and frivolous exercise of "I got options" that calls sacrifice a disgrace that prompts premature dissolutions of families and accounts for much of the misery in our society today. The modern application of sacrifice involves institutionalizing babies in childcare and elders in rest homes while citing the willingness to work additional hours to upgrade the institution as the ultimate sacrifice. It's akin to making the contribution of the chicken's egg to the breakfast menu on par with the sacrifice of the hog's bacon to the breakfast menu. One can be achieved in less than a day's work, and the other requires total commitment.

The strength of my mother's commitment and sacrifice is evident by the endless value of my inheritance that I extend to this and every other generation to eternity. It is my mother's sacrifice that I salute and honor. In the shadow of her sacrifice, I rise and take a bow.

# Final Thoughts

Because of all the abuse my father exacted on the entire family, including my mother, I constantly asked myself, "How did you respect your father?" In the end, I am able to understand that both my father and mother loved their children and wanted the best for them. My father was driven by fear and chose to use what he knew—brute force on his boys, a lesser level of force on his girls, and intimidation on his girls' boyfriends—as his guarantee that we would stay out of trouble and stay on the right path of life. It was madness with a purpose.

My mother was driven by faith, faith in my father that he would have the strength and fortitude to provide that toughness that she thought we needed from time to time, even though she cringed as he administered it. Most importantly, she had faith in God with the understanding that there was only One who provided the ultimate guarantee, and she would have the common sense and discipline to get out the way and let God do His job. My mother's peace, calmness, and quietness were proof that, no matter what was going on, God was still in control, and her faith was in that guarantee.

*The End.*

# Index

In the Shadow of Sacrifice: Thoughts on Life and Success is a memoir and collection of essays—often humorous but always thought-provoking. It presents a literary portrait of the author's life journey to not just overcome but rise above stuttering, poverty, illiteracy, under-nourishment, the abusive disciplinary methods of his father, and the excessive application of the village concept from his older siblings and the community.

The variety awakens the senses by rhythmically undulating between heartrending exposés, dark and light-hearted comical interludes, and quite pensive introspections that deliver the inspirational themes that, *your stumbling blocks are just launching pads*; and *challenges are merely masking as physical impediments, designed to ignite your mental processes, strengthen and clarify your purpose, heighten your determination, and crystallize your resolve.*

Both inspired and driven by the sacrifices of the author's mother, In The Shadow of Sacrifice: Thoughts on Life and Success is as a tribute to his mother and all mothers who protect and often surrender their total being for the hope of a promising future for their children.

mL   2·15